BEFORE THE ECHO

NUMBER TWENTY-EIGHT
CORRIE HERRING HOOKS SERIES

Before the Echo

ESSAYS ON NATURE
BY PETE DUNNE

DRAWINGS BY DIANA MARLINSKI

UNIVERSITY OF TEXAS PRESS, AUSTIN

Requests for permission to reproduce material
from this work should be sent to
Permissions, University of Texas Press,
Box 7819, Austin, Texas 78713-7819.

⊗ The paper used in this publication meets
the minimum requirements of American National Standard
for Information Sciences—Permanence of Paper
for Printed Library Materials, ANSI Z39.48-1984.

LIBRARY OF CONGRESS
CATALOGING-IN-PUBLICATION DATA

Dunne, Pete, 1951–
    Before the echo : essays on nature / Pete Dunne. — 1st ed.
        p.   cm. — (Corrie Herring Hooks series ; no. 28)
    ISBN 0-292-71578-1
    1. Natural history.   2. Nature.   3. Nature
conservation.
I. Title.   II. Series.
QH81.D837   1995
508—dc20   94-22910

This one's for Linda

Contents

Acknowledgments

WRITING is not as singular an endeavor as some might believe. There were writers who came before who inspired; there were friends along the way who added the weight of their counsel and support.

By defining narrowly those individuals whose names warrant inclusion here, it is not my intention to diminish the influence of, or my gratitude toward, those many others who have figured in these writings. My purpose, rather, is to offer special recognition, in the humble manner of a scribe, to those who by their special contributions have already distinguished themselves.

My special thanks then,

To: Richard Roberts, Fletcher Roberts, Robert Stock, Gloria Saffron, and Ernie Solis of the *New York Times*; Nancy Simmons of *Wildlife Conservation*; and Evan Cutler of *Countryside Magazine* for editorial counsel;

To: Jim Carmichel and John Barsness for interrupting their busy schedules to offer sage advice concerning the essay "Spent Shot Shell";

To: Friends Jay Darling, Victor Emanuel, Paul Kerlinger, Rick Radis, Dale Rosselet, the late Floyd Wolfarth, Tom and Debi Zeno, and nephew Kevin Dunne, who figured in or were the inspiration for essays included in this collection;

To: Dorothy Clair, my very special editorial overlord, and Don Frieday, naturalist, writer, and friend, who has more than once played the role of writer's sounding board and who stands, as I do, before the echo; and, of course,

To: My wife, Linda, who has already been introduced to you in the pages of this book, but who figures in everything.

Preface: Musical Chairs

THERE WAS A GAME we used to play back in grade school—maybe they still do. It was the teacher's safety valve for rainy day lunches; the graphite rod that dampened pre-vacation energy levels. It was called "musical chairs." This is how it worked.

Two rows of chairs would be lined up, back to back. The class would form a line that circled the empty seats. Then the teacher would put a record on the phonograph (they didn't have CD players yet) and play a song. When the music started, the class would march; when it stopped everyone would scramble for a chair.

There was a catch, of course. There weren't enough chairs to go around. Someone was always left standing. That meant having to leave the game.

It was lots of fun, musical chairs. Except when you lost.

The natural world is a lot like this. Nature calls the tune and the great journey begins—from birth to death; across the interlocking web of living things whose strands serve as our planetary safety net and whose borders define existence. Everywhere you turn, everywhere you go, there are places where living things sit down, niches that support their specific needs. But, just as in musical chairs, there aren't enough places to go around. Our species keeps removing them— forcing other creatures to leave the game.

I am a writer and I am an environmentalist, one who has worked most of his adult life for the New Jersey Audubon

Society and whose writings have tried to forge a link between people and the natural world. In your hand is a select culling of the best and the brightest of those essays—the ones that have found a place in my esteem and will, I hope, in yours.

Many of these essays were written to impart under-standing; others to point out flaws in our species' regard for the environment. A few are flights of fancy, essays that use nature to explore situations that are very human—human and funny; human and troubled, as I and other environmen-tally sensitive people are sometimes troubled.

Troubled that the equatorial forests, the very center-piece of nature's web, are being lost on my generation's watch; troubled that the river of the migratory songbirds that passes my door has been reduced to a trickle; troubled that creatures as grand as tigers and as unobtrusive as frogs and salamanders are being pushed past the rim of existence; troubled that those who are united in their support for the natural world are too often divided by their means of inter-action to the environment's great loss.

"So," you are thinking, "this is another one of those doom and gloom environmental books?" Oh, no. Quite the contrary. This is a very optimistic book. Its essays were ex-pressly written to entertain readers and to make the natural world real, not threatening. Most of the essays in this collec-tion originate from my regular column in the New Jersey Sun-day Section of the *New York Times* and, as such, are written to appeal to a general readership, because . . .

Because we have come to live in a society that has grown increasingly estranged from nature, you and I. Once familiar things, like the stars and the tides, are alien now. The light of fireflies and the death of hunted things, familiar tenets of our ancestors' world, have been relegated to society's storehouse of ignorance.

And ignorance has a sinister twin, unmindfulness. It is one thing for a creature to be unaware of the consequences of its actions. It's quite another to forge ahead as if we were aware—calling our own self-serving tune in the high stakes game of musical chairs, grabbing all the spaces, turning a blind eye to the host of creatures being forced to leave the game. But that is what is happening. And that is the flaw in our approach to this world that the essays in this collection address.

Humanity and nature *will* strike a balance someday. It is inevitable and it is natural. The questions are, at what point *and* what measure of our natural heritage will remain when humans and environment do finally come to terms. The answer will determine nothing less than what kind of world we will live in—and it might determine whether we live at all.

For my part, I'd strike that balance sooner rather than later, while most of the earth's riches are still on the table and we are capable of this.

If we use the deductive powers that our species is so proud of.

If we accept the premise that nature is not a competing interest among many but the foundation upon which all other interests compete.

If we are wise.

Then you and I and the generations that follow will continue to enjoy a world of marvelous complexity and one in which all living things are accorded a place.

And if we fail?

Then when the game is over, and all other creatures have left the game, I wonder how we are going to feel about claiming our prize. The last chair, in an empty room.

—Pete Dunne
Cape May Point, N.J.
March 1994

BEFORE THE ECHO

Barely, New Jersey

MOST EVENINGS, on my way home from New Jersey Audubon's Scherman-Hoffman Sanctuary, I run just ahead of the wave of I-78 commuters, struggling to hold my place among all those other productive members of the work force. Every exit siphons off cars until just past Clinton, when the congestion eases somewhat. First one, then another driver accelerates, racing to put the workday behind. An increase of just five miles per hour can add minutes to a body's minimum daily allotment of Quality Time. And Quality Time in this day and age is a commodity too precious to waste.

This far out, most metro commuters enjoy their QT over in Pennsylvania. Me? I still live in New Jersey. Barely, New Jersey. If you've never heard of it, I'm not surprised.

"Barely" isn't a town. Barely is as much a state of mind as a place. What does it look like? Well, Barely is sort of open and lush and hilly and wooded, and farms are not the exception. There are no traffic lights in Barely. No strip malls. No traffic patterns that negate themselves. There is air you don't mind breathing, water you don't second guess, and at night even the lesser stars shine down on Barely.

Not so long ago, Barely had another name. It was called Mostly. But twenty years of uncontrolled growth and development changed all that. Now, Mostly is history and Barely is barely found in New Jersey.

Yep, Barely, New Jersey. A wonderful place with a fine history and an uncertain future. You'd like it.

Just before the exit to Barely, there is a hill. From the top of that hill, at the point you catch your first glimpse of forested hillside, it's just five minutes to my driveway. For four years, my eyes preyed on that hillside. Just gazing at it added two minutes of QT to my day.

Then, one afternoon after returning from a period of travel, I crested the hill, turned expectant eyes upon Barely, and realized that its integrity had been shattered. There, blighting Barely's landscape, was a stunningly ugly corporate building.

Note, I did not say corporate headquarters. There was no corporate banner flying out front, no occupying business to breathe life into the shell. The building was unoccupied then. It is, four years later as I rework these essays for this book, unoccupied now—a singularly ugly building mantling a hillside where trees and fields used to be.

Was there anything unique about that hillside? No, it was just a nice hillside that had the ill fortune to be zoned commercial on some map. Were there any "threatened" or "endangered" species on it? No, not as far as I know.

There were just a few songbirds—yellow warblers, blue-winged warblers, a chestnut-sided warbler . . . maybe a golden-winged.

There were, predictably enough, black snakes, box turtles, painted ladies, crickets, praying mantis, and who knows how many deer mice. There was undoubtedly a ground hog. There might have been a red fox den. There were certainly deer.

There were all these things, and many more, and now they have been replaced by an empty building nobody wants (including the bank that may assume it and the taxpayers who could ultimately get stuck with the tab).

Now, I am not an intelligent man, and I am economically illiterate, to boot. I temporarily store whatever money is left over at the end of the month in a bank (to the horror of my investment-something-or-other brother-in-law). I define a "commodity" as something I keep in my closet, and "future" is something that starts tomorrow.

I tell you this so you will understand why I fail to understand why anybody would destroy a hillside in order to put up a building nobody wants.

I could understand if it was just a mistake. Say somebody ordered the building, and it was the wrong color, and then they didn't like it. But in my travels around my state, I have seen many office buildings and half-built condominiums and lonely model homes on razed sites. All of these structures are there at the expense of wildlife and habitat and the natural environment, and all of them are empty.

All these structures can't be the wrong color, can they?

I took my question to my investment-something-or-other brother-in-law, who explained that what had happened was that all these projects had been started on speculation and that then the economy had slumped and that now nobody wanted them.

I asked him whether he thought that was right.

He asked me whether I thought "what was right."

I asked him whether he thought it was right that people should be allowed to just go out and level natural areas on nothing more substantial than speculation.

He asked me whether I was some sort of Communist.

I said I didn't think I was a Communist because I'm just as opposed to people building things that don't work as I am to people building things nobody wants. I said I didn't think I was a Communist because Communists believed in history, and I was trying to maintain some faint faith in the future.

But, as I said, I'm not an intelligent man.

I'm also not a very political man, which may explain why I don't have a better grasp of political philosophies. But I made it a point to listen to my governor's state of the state address one January—the January after the ugly corporate building was built. All those empty office buildings on all those denuded lots were beginning to distress me, and I was curious to see whether anyone in government was as concerned about them as I was.

As it turned out, there was a great deal of concern. But my grasp of the problem proved faulty again. I thought that the problem with the state was that there were too many buildings. The real problem, it turns out, was that there weren't enough buildings—a shortfall, our governor explained, that could be amended by spurring growth and development.

To me, this sounded a little like being in a hole and trying to get out by digging harder and faster. But as I said before, I'm not an intelligent man.

Even people from Barely who are not very intelligent have the right to ask questions (which is certainly better than relying on people who are not very intelligent to answer questions), so I have a question I'd like to ask. It's the question an architect asks when he contemplates the design for a new corporate headquarters. It's the question a Michelangelo might have posed when he stood in front of a piece of marble, planted his chisel, raised his hammer, and tried to conjure the image of David. It's the question God might have asked when he made the earth.

The question is this: What do we want places like New Jersey to look like when they are finished? Do we want them to be a schizophrenic patchwork and a traffic corridor for people traveling from their homes that are one place and jobs that are someplace else? Or do we want them to be places where people choose to live? Someplace like Barely.

Barely, New Jersey.

Common Ground

THE SKUNK paused when it reached the edge of the woods, puzzled and cautious. Last year in March, when it had emerged from hibernation, there had been a woodland here. Now, nine months later, there was a landscape scraped clean of vegetation, festooned with structures flanking macadam strips. The strips bore names like oak, sycamore, beech—a subtle touch of irony that the skunk would probably have enjoyed (if skunks could read). As it was, the street signs meant as little to this docile, even-tempered member of the weasel clan as the bloom of orange survey tape had meant the previous spring.

Skunks are not noted for their intellect, although they can exhibit an admirable single-mindedness about some things—like winter dens. But cerebral or not, skunks can generally play a winning hand with the cards that they've been dealt. Animals that test the limits of a skunk's good nature usually don't do so twice. There are two exceptions to this general rule.

One is the great-horned owl. They eat skunks. The other is the automobile. They hit them. If someone asks you what owls and automobiles have in common, now you know. They both have a poorly developed sense of smell.

The skunk, who thus far had avoided both owls and autos, enjoyed a very acute sense of smell, and he was, at this very moment, putting this gift to use. The night air carried a cornucopia of intriguing odors—the wholesome reek of fresh cut lumber, spilled diesel fuel, discarded cigarettes, lawn fertilizer, Anne Taylor's prowling tabby, and the leftover chicken in the garbage bag sitting on Bob O'Mally's curb. The skunk homed in on the O'Mally property. This was where it had been heading anyway. The chicken was a bonus.

Like a piebald shadow, the animal ambled across a landscape that looked as if it had been tortured—past poured foundations, frames with roofs, frames without roofs, houses with discarded wiring and sheetrock piled out front, and finally houses with cars parked in their driveways. In fields or woodlands, the skunk would have moved with more care. Its senses would have been on the alert for cold-numbed crickets or mice made frantic and incautious by winter's imminence. But the embryonic development was pretty sterile from a dietary standpoint. And besides, chicken in the can is worth any number of crickets out in the bush.

The animal paused briefly in the shadow of a streetlight when Frank Delia's shepherd caught wind of the intruder and started to bark its head off. But fortune smiled on Frank and his shepherd. The chain held.

Thirty seconds later and two doors up, some sixth sense made Anne Taylor's tabby withdraw her head from the violated forty-gallon trash bag, the opposing ends of a freshly salvaged chicken wing protruding from her mouth. The sight of twelve pounds of male skunk, four feet away, served to compromise her sense of accomplishment and undermine her usual feline composure.

Anne Taylor's tabby might not have been the brightest cat on earth, but when it came to skunks, she was in the upper percentile of her graduating class. When the skunk danced a threatening little jig with its front paws, tabby modified her opening position by dropping the chicken wing and running like hell. Oh, tabby remembered skunks all right.

And so does Anne!

For that matter, so does Anne's bridge club.

The skunk dined leisurely on chicken garnished with fruit salad and coffee grounds. The casserole of opportunity *might* have benefitted from a bit less clam dip (but this was really a minor point—nothing to call to the management's attention). Dinner completed, the skunk ambled up the blacktop driveway heading for the location of its old den under the windblown tree—the one that used to be right where Bob's garage was now. It paused at the open door.

The place had certainly changed. The skunk made its way past an eclectic assortment of hardware, hoses, and shipping boxes that had yet to be unpacked. It scratched at the hard concrete right where it felt certain that the entrance used to be.

Puzzled, the skunk coursed beneath the somewhat overprized symbol of Bob's promotion, sniffed the wheels, and, frustrated, began a reconnaissance in search of the opening to its misplaced den. It certainly was a puzzle. In fact, it was quite irritating.

It was too late to search for a better place for the night, so the skunk settled for the half cord of firewood stacked along the back wall. There proved to be a nice snug place be-

tween the stacks that would serve in the short run. It wasn't perfect. It wasn't a proper den. But it would have to do.

It *certainly* was *irritating*. In fact, it was downright *annoying*. Its disposition thoroughly soured by circumstance, the skunk settled in for a nap.

Some days are just bad days, and that's all there is to it. Bob knew it was going to be "one of those . . ." as soon as the clock radio went off in his ear, making a noise like a locomotive in free fall (clear evidence that his teenage daughter had been taking liberties with the phone in their room, again).

He lurched into the bathroom (congratulating himself for remembering that the door on *this* bathroom was on rollers—not on hinges like the one in the old house (or as he had put it to his wife and later the repairman "like a normal house").

After a ferocious battle with a shower that seemed to have no setting at a temperature that would support life, he tackled the rest of the morning ritual, discovering, in ascending order of importance, that it is important to check to see whether the cap is tight *before* lifting the bottle of vitamins, that underarm deodorant had been left off the shopping list, and that unless the light switch by the door is moved to the "on" position, razors left overnight to recharge, don't.

He used his wife's deodorant and the razor that lived in the shower. Needless to say, he nicked himself. Twice.

It took only four tries before he located the cabinet that housed the coffee mugs (one above par) but six attempts before he finally located the coffee (a double bogie). He didn't even try to guess which drawer hid the flatware, electing instead to rummage through the dishwasher and salvage a clean spoon from the rack.

Well, it was *almost* clean.

"Moving into a new place is such a pain," he thought irritably. "Nothing is where it should be. Nothing comes easy. You have to think and plan every single thing you do."

"It's a wonder human beings didn't just stay in their caves," he muttered.

Over coffee that came out weak, he studied notes for the

oral presentation he was to make that morning. This was a big one. His new department head and the president of the division would be there, and he wanted to make an impression. This one was *very* big.

It wasn't until he'd finished his coffee that he discovered the clam dip all over the bottom of his tie.

The car started grudgingly, the price of having left the garage door open when he'd put the garbage out the night before. Diesel engines, even diesel engines of German descent, are not winter Olympians by choice.

While he let the engine warm, he cast an appraising eye over the car, searching for any blemish or flaw in the spotless interior. He didn't expect to find any. The car was barely a week old.

Bob's supervisor had hinted that lunch with the vice-president was a distinct possibility after the meeting. So Bob was going to work early, to get a parking spot close to the main entrance, to put himself in the best position to drive.

He put the car in gear, and as the car edged out of the garage, Bob felt a bump. Not a big bump. Just a bump—like the rear wheel running over something.

"Damn," he thought. "Damn. Now what? Nothing in its place. Everything out of order. Just one Goddamn annoyance after another."

He got out to find out what garden tool would have to be replaced but found instead a complimentary copy of the regional newspaper. Holding his other best tie with one hand, he salvaged the paper with the other. The headline read: WINTER ARRIVES TODAY! The first paragraph promised arctic air and temperatures in the twenties by nightfall.

As he put the car in reverse, again, it occurred to him that the outside water lines hadn't been turned off, yet. Indecision reigned for only a moment. Bob O'Mally was someone who had a reputation for getting things done.

Putting the car in neutral, he eased himself out of the door, and being careful not to brush up against anything with his trousers, he slipped between the fender and bags of fertilizer and made his way toward the shutoff valve just behind the stack of firewood.

Nothing but the Wind

THE CLOUDS began to move, slowly at first, gaining momentum by degrees. Here and there moonlight probed for weak points, nibbling at the seams of the dark gray mass.

A victorious star appeared, but the clouds rallied, closing the gap in their ranks. Another peaked though momentarily and then another, *there . . .* and *there . . .* and *there . . .*

On the far side of the pond, newly glazed by the rain that froze as it fell, ice-sheathed limbs began to tremble. The sound of wind in branches increased until the night air was filled with the sound of branches at odds with the wind—and the brittle sound of ice falling to earth.

The fox was hungry and a bit out of sorts—peeved, actually. The ice-rain that had fallen half the night had kept it den-bound—along with every mouse, shrew, and vole in the world it seemed. The ice had put a fox-resistant crust over the rodent runs. He couldn't smell a freaking thing. And now, *now* the wind was blowing to beat the band!

"The *mus* tabernacle choir could stand in my left ear belting out arias, and I couldn't hear them," he thought bleakly. This wasn't, strictly speaking, true, but it made him feel better to complain. In fact, five minutes later, he was listening intently to an argument between two meadow voles involving navigation rights in an upper-level rodent run. The issue was settled by outside arbitration.

The wind was also a matter of concern for the young buck cottontail rabbit. Rabbits, too, are not particularly happy about wind. It masks the effectiveness of their prime defense mechanism—their hypersensitive ears. And though hungry, the rabbit had no intention of venturing out of the protective confines of the greenbrier tangle into a world that sounded like an imploding china shop.

The rabbit moved cautiously beneath the canopy of living barbed wire that was its home, straining to reach the tender branches that had survived the reach of smaller rabbits. Later in the season, these would be gone too, and the rabbit would have to follow the lead of less burly members of the clan who were already foraging widely, despite the risk.

Risk, spelled o w l, was not having a splendid night, either. He and the missus had been working themselves into a pretty fair romantic mood for the past couple of weeks. Great-horned owls are slow starters, and courtship is a protracted affair—even between couples of long standing.

Vocalizations play a key role in reestablishing the pair bond (which is to say, they talk a lot first). And it's tough discussing intimate concerns, hopes for the future, and whether you prefer nesting on the abandoned (or very soon to be abandoned) squirrel nest or atop the ol' hollow tree when it's blowing a gale.

One of their concerns, the one involving nest site selection, was in the process of solving itself by default. The hollow tree, the battered remains of what had once been a splendid white oak, had survived years of adversity: high winds and heavy snows, boring beetles and chisel-billed woodpeckers, penknives wielded by young hands, random lightning bolts, and, of course, wood stoves that needed filling. But the end was at hand.

The tree had recently served as the epicenter for teenage beer parties in the grove. The ceremonial fire had worked hand in hand with the natural processes of deterioration to weaken the tree's long-standing resolve. The heavy mantle of ice and the winds that raked the forest were the last straw. With a shudder and a crack, the proud monarch started down.

Meanwhile, halfway up, in a cavity opening on the south side, a somewhat groggy raccoon was trying to come to grips with what, to his mind, was a very surprising turn

of events. Two doors up and on the right, the family of flying squirrels was scrambling an evacuation. In something under two seconds, four saucer-eyed rodents exited from three
holes, streaking across the party glen like furry Frisbees.

Two landed dead on target, one caught a backup branch,
the fourth, failing to allow for windage, shot wide of the mark
and hit the forest floor.

Flying squirrels lose points for touching the ground.
Trees, on the other hand, do not, and with a resounding
crash, the tree, which remembered New Jersey when it was
chartered by a king, executed a magnificent belly flop. Several hundred pounds of ice went spinning off as shards of
moonlight.

Overhead, beyond the bowed heads of trees, a flock of
tundra swans fled south, pushed by gale force winds. The
birds had lingered on a national wildlife refuge farther north,
but the cold, cold air that would follow the wind had forced
them on. Though fast flyers, the swans could not have at-
tained their one-hundred-mile-per-hour cruising speed were
it not for the friendly tail wind. Their destination was North
Carolina. They would be there by sunrise.

In a grape and honeysuckle tangle, a white-throated
sparrow slept fitfully. The bird was cold, wet and cold. Its
energy needs had forced it to feed in the rain before going to
roost, and in the process it had gotten wet.

Wet feathers are poor insulators. The bird tried to find a
place that offered some escape from the heat-leaching wind
that seemed to pour through the honeysuckle from a million
places at once. The food it had taken in was gone. Dawn was
still several hours away. The bird began to shiver.

But the otters had never had so much fun. The world
was one big friction-free playground, and the fivesome, four
siblings and their mother, were having a wonderful time nav-
igating the ice-glazed marsh, falling onto their sides, watching the world go by. The wind whipping across the open flats
was a bonus. It gave them just the extra little push they
needed to sustain a good, long glide.

But when the traveling circus reached the banks of the
river that was the heart of their tidal domain, they almost

suffered enthusiasm-induced seizures. The tug of the moon had pulled the ocean's water away from the land—but the wind, the wind howling across Delaware Bay, had dropped the tide to an all-time low. Given the nature of land and water, if you take away the water what you are left with is . . .

Mud! Mile after luscious mile of what the experts unanimously proclaim is some of the finest, slickest sliding mud in the world—good old Delaware Bay blue mud. In something under ten seconds, five of the world's top mud testers were hard at play.

In the bay, mussel beds that had never felt the killing touch of air were tightening their hatches against a harsh, new reality. In the shipping lane, rafts of scaup tightened ranks, kept their keels into the wind, and slept.

On the lee side of the coastal jetties, hardy sea ducks huddled against the protecting wall of rock. On every coastal beach, smooth, round grains of sand tumbled mindlessly into the breakers, a process called erosion. On the Kittatinny Ridge, a mountain ash was stripped of the last few berries left to it. One tumbled into a fertile pocket out of the reach of small foraging paws.

On the bedroom balcony of a condominium whose main selling point was the unobstructed view, a ceramic wind chime, a souvenir from a trip to Monterey, California, finally gave up its heroic struggle and surrendered to gravity.

"What was that?" the startled mother of two whispered into the darkness.

"Ummmmm," the form lying next to her suggested, but "ummmm" wasn't the right answer. Seconds passed and the world did not.

"Did you hear that noise?" she demanded.

Both of them listened for signs that the world was not as it should be.

"It's nothing," her sleepy spouse pronounced, finally. "Nothing but the wind."

It took half an hour, but the dazed and not terribly happy raccoon finally found a snug corner beneath a stream-cut bank. It wasn't perfect, but at least it was out of the wind.

Babes in the Woods

Shhhhh. There're babes in the woods—and the prairies and the mountaintops; huddled on tundra hillsides and crouched creekside in southern swamps. All across America, new life is peeking out, taking its first look at a world filled with discovery . . . and *danger*.

Acting as a buffer between young innocence and a hostile world is a maternal filter that lets reality pass to the next generation gradually—not in a killing rush. This is Mom, and whether the kids like it or not, she'll be the one calling the shots for a while.

It is certain that the new generation will use every means at their disposal to put themselves in harm's way—will thrust questioning noses at buzzing rattlesnakes, ignore the warning shadow of a hunting eagle, tempt gravity beyond the limits of friction and balance. And although young animals are not defenseless, come into life, like young bobcats, cryptically colored or, like young porcupines, wearing an arsenal on their backs, when the chips are down, Mom is the first line of defense. They can be confident that she will use all the survival skills gathered on the road to maturity to protect them. That's what mothers are for.

Have you ever wondered why baby animals strike such warm chords in us? Why a kitten in the picture makes product sales jump. Why Bambi has stolen a billion hearts. Why the portrait of a baby harp seal makes urban-hardened hearts melt and animal protectionists militant.

Baby horned toads and baby caterpillars don't elicit this response. Yet if you study the puss of a baby harp seal and the anterior end of a banded woollybear caterpillar, you'll not fail to note a remarkable similarity.

Maybe it's the vulnerability young animals expose to the hurtful ills of the world. It pierces our emotional shell, makes us protective of them, releases those maternal (and paternal) instincts. Remember, we are animals. We have babes, too.

Maybe in some nostalgic way, young animals recall our own childhoods, that careless, free-for-all time (before mortgages) when wonder was found in the wing of a butterfly, challenge meant catching bullfrogs, and life held no greater threat than wet sneakers (and a mother's admonishment).

Or maybe we are moved by their innocence. Adult foxes (and bobcats and mountain goats) avoid us, fear us, put distance between us. But kits (. . . and kittens . . . and kids . . .), knowing nothing of our species' capriciousness, do not. Wait patiently, and young foxes soon fill the entrance of their den with curious faces; kids, all stiff-legged and nose-twitching, edge across a scree-strewn slope for a better look.

They seem to "trust us," appreciate us for the good-natured creatures we believe ourselves to be. We return the compliment with affection.

It doesn't matter, and it rarely occurs to us while we watch them at their play, that little foxes and little bobcats grow up to become thinking, calculating, killing creatures. That while young predators play, they are honing skills that they will use to open the throats of deer and reduce live rabbits to scraps of fur and bloody slush.

Our minds recoil from the realization that nursing deer mice and nursing fox kits will one day be bound in a ritual of recycling called predation. We choose to forget (if we ever knew) that most of the young born in any given year do not live to produce young of their own, that what we regard as fragile and precious, nature calls "interchangeable parts," and that dying is just as *natural* as living—merely different.

We fasten instead upon the young and their season, and why not? Just because summer and youth and innocence do not last, does not mean that they are not real or that we should not be moved by babes in the woods.

Before the Echo

WHEN I WAS YOUNG, I was a hunter, walked wooded hillsides with confident steps and a gun in my hands. I knew the blur of wings, the rocketing form, and the Great Moment that only hunters know, when all existence draws down to two points and a single line.

And the universe holds its breath.

And what may be and what will be meet and become one . . .

Before the echo returns to its source.

The woods, *my* woods, lay behind my parents' house and were typical of New Jersey woodlots—second-growth tangles wrapped in catbrier where rabbits made trails in the snow, stands of oak and hickory rich in wild grape and wildly flushing grouse. Some owner's stubbornness defended these acres from development. Some patience beyond the call of parenthood allowed me to wander them at will—with binoculars in spring and summer while lawns went uncut, with a shotgun in autumn and winter while homework went undone.

Through binoculars I learned the skills that would lead me to my craft—the craft of professional birder. I learned the lore of wing bars and tail spots. I studied the raptorial specks and conjured names for them. I watched the hosts of migrating shorebirds and built identifications for them from scratch.

With the shotgun I gained wisdom and understanding and a harvest of memories that have lasted a lifetime.

There was the day, after the echo had passed, that I reached a trembling hand into the leaves and lifted a rabbit still warm as life and knew, and felt, and thought . . .

"I did this."

There was the drake wood duck, spawned by a misty dawn, that folded its wings at the report of my gun and arrowed into the lake without ripple or sound. I stripped and swam to retrieve that bird, then carried it home in cradling arms so as not to spoil its feathers. Later, with the bird spread upon my desk—beside the homework that would not get done—I wondered how *anything* could be so beautiful.

There was the red fox slung over my shoulder the way I once saw such a thing depicted in a painting by Winslow Homer, that stopped rush hour traffic along Old Troy Road, and drew the praise and the hands of strangers. My clothes were stained to the undergarments with blood by the time I reached home, and once again I stared and wondered at the stilled life that had been absorbed and become part of mine.

With these tools, the binocular and the shotgun, I grew intimate with my woods. I came to know it, and all that live in it, the way a predator knows its territory, and my confidence grew in measure with my skills. This is what it takes to be an accomplished field birder. This is what it takes to hunt with confidence and clear purpose.

You will think, perhaps, that you see a contradiction here. You will wonder, maybe, how it can be that a person can both appreciate wild, living things and kill them, too?

Yes, I see your dilemma, and I've faced this question before from strangers and friends, in discussions with co-workers, and at dinner parties where conversations turn serious and where truth is served. And there *is* an answer, if you'll have it—an imperfect one.

Think of the natural world as a great play, an incredible drama held on a world stage in which all living things play a part. When I carry binoculars, I stand with the audience, an omniscient observer to all that goes on around me, and I enjoy this very much. But when I carry a gun, I become an actor, *become part of the play itself.* This I relish, too.

But as I said, the answer is imperfect. It strikes deep into reason but misses the heart.

There is another answer—one that draws closer to the truth but in doing so becomes enigmatic and inexplicable. I cannot formulate this answer. I can tell you only where you might find it for yourself.

The answer lies after the shot and before the echo. It can be heard only by those who stand in the echo's path. But this answer, that lasts only as long as an echo, is complete.

I hunted through high school. I hunted through college and into early manhood. I hunted right up to that morning in December when the line of my sight joined the point of my gun to the point that lies behind the foreleg of a deer—the place where its life is housed.

I recall how the animal stopped where my will said "stop." I remember how my finger found the trigger and how the cold touch of it set the world trembling.

I remember how the animal stood.

How the Great Moment came.

How the Universe held its breath, waiting . . . waiting . . . for the sound of an echo that never returned. The echo of a shot that was never fired.

Maybe it was the orange survey tape that was blooming throughout my woodlands, sapping my resolve, usurping my territory, forcing me to hunt elsewhere, without standing or confidence.

Maybe it was the compounded uncertainties of that age. A president shot in Dallas. A brother who would be president dead in Los Angeles. A nation whose faith was being bled away by a conflict in Asia.

Maybe it was the uncertainties of *my* age—that confused period in a person's life when questions are more common than answers, and things that were must be set aside to make room for things that might be.

For whatever reason, my heart and mind were no longer aligned along the barrel of a gun. My resolve had been breached, and without conviction, hunting is a pantomime, hunting is a *sham!* And a person who cannot hunt with conviction should not hunt at all.

So I put my gun away and found my place in the audience. I never stopped being a hunter, maybe. But I did stop hunting—until the day, should it ever come, that the right-ness returned.

For nearly two decades now, my life has been directed toward fostering an appreciation of the natural world. From a distance, I have heard the war of words waged between those who defended hunting and those who decried it. Listened to the arguments mouthed by sportsmen—banal truths about "controlling the herd" and "harvesting the surplus" and "maintaining the balance" as if hunting were some sort of civic-minded cleanup.

That's not why they hunted. I knew that. Maybe they could not articulate their reason and so retreated behind the defensive arguments erected by game management engineers. But that's still not why they hunted, and their rhetoric bridged no gaps and did no service to the truth.

I heard the arguments fostered by the gun lobby who claimed that they represented my interest but whose extremist stand against sensible legislation made me ashamed to own firearms. I puzzled over the bumper stickers that reminded me that guns, guts, and God were part of an American Trinity; that guns didn't kill people (bullets do, right?); and that the owner of the vehicle ahead of me would sooner leave his wife than give up his gun.

And I wondered what *any* of this nonsense had to do with hunting?

I listened to the impassioned accusations of antihunters who believe that hunting is synonymous with killing and that anyone who hunts is unfeeling and cruel. These people, at least, were not dishonest. They were sensitive people who felt pain as if it were their own and were moved to stop it. They said what they felt and believed.

No, they weren't dishonest. They were merely wrong, and I had standing to judge. I knew, where they could only guess, what hunting was, and I know that hunting is no more killing than the death of Julius Caesar is Shakespeare's play.

I *knew* where they could only *guess* what my feelings were, and I know that I am neither unfeeling nor cruel. If they feel the pain, *I* have felt the death!

I have stood in the moment before the echo. They have not.

Twenty years I heard the arguments. Weighed the words. Felt the conflict both within and without. And during that time, I built a life, battled to keep orange flags at bay, schooled the public in the importance of protecting the natural world, and grew, as people do, in confidence and skill.

And in these last few years, as my life has approached midspan, a strange thing has happened, a thing I did not expect. More and more I found myself paying heed to the chorus of geese on still autumn nights—found myself rising from my chair, edging onto the porch, turning my eyes to the sky and my mind upon memories.

If while walking some woodland path, I chanced to find a spent shot shell I would reach into the leaves, cradle the empty casing in my hands, and attempt to reconstruct the drama that had unfolded here—try to find names for the actors that had taken part in this ancient play.

And if, as sometimes happened, a grouse flushed from beside the trail, a secret part of me would measure the distance. Judge the angle. Gauge the speed. And estimate, based upon reflexes that exist only in memory, what my chances might have been.

I realized one evening, after the bird had gone, after the leaves had settled, after I had stood for what must have been a very long time, that I was waiting for something. A half-forgotten sound. A memory. An echo.

So it came to be, it came to pass, that one day last autumn I picked up my gun, and I went hunting—excused myself from the audience and took up, once again, my old part, on a new stage, in drama I recall so well. I hunted all day with confidence, and when the Great Moment came discovered that both my heart and my mind were aligned as truly as a line drawn between two points. I fired twice.

With what results?

The answer to that lies between me and the echo.

Cast of Stars

WE WERE standing on the observation deck of The Arc, stop one on the Kenyan Safari circuit, and it was dark, very dark because it was night as night should be.

"What's that?" a middle-aged member of my tour group whispered, pointing skyward. She had a voice that discarded consonants but got the most out of vowels—a New Yorker's voice.

"What's what?" I asked, aligning my eyes along her upraised arm, finding nothing out of the ordinary—nothing but more points of light than even a presidential speech writer can conjure.

"That," she said, not whispering now, but my puzzlement only increased.

"*That*," she repeated, giving in to exasperation. "That . . . that . . . *glow* in the sky. What is it?"

With a sad shock, I realized, finally, what it was that the woman was referring to. Maybe she saw me shudder, maybe not, and it's possible, very possible, that she wouldn't have even understood how deeply I was troubled by her tragic disclosure.

"That," I said in my most controlled voice, "is the Milky Way."

The road went from pitted macadam to pocked dirt. Flanking walls of trees fell away to be replaced by open marsh. I was about as far from a town as you can be in New

Jersey, and a glance through the windshield confirmed that it was far enough—just enough. The sky overhead was a star-studded dome whose rim was the horizon. I parked. Got out of my car. Turned. And faced the universe.

I am not going to lie to you and offer myself as some sort of astrological Einstein. Fact is, I'm hardly more constellation conversant than your average person, can't tell Pisces from Picadilly, and can barely find Andromeda on a map. I'm very much a product of my time.

Oh, I'm grounded in the basics, able to identify some of the megafauna of the night sky. I can nail Orion at a glance, and, lining up along the hunter's belt, I can peg Taurus the bull. The Seven Sisters, the Pleiades cluster, live right next door.

Give me half a minute and half a turn, and I'll usually manage to find the big dipper. After a little trial and error, I'll recall which of the constellation's stars you line your sight along to locate Polaris, the North Star. With this star to guide me, with a cold clear night, I can conjure Ursa Minor (often as not).

But give or take a few planets and stars, that's where my familiarity with the night sky ends. And this is very sad. This is something that should never have been let to happen.

Once, before VCRs, before Vanna White, the earth was populated by a wonderful creative people. They lived wherever landmasses could be found. They spoke many languages, had different cultures, enjoyed different traditions, worshipped different gods. What they had in common was their imaginations and their familiarity with the night sky.

Winter nights were just as long before the invention of picture tubes as they are now. So after dinner and a busy day of hunting and gathering or tilling the crops, these imaginative people would kick back, free their minds of the cares of the day, and fasten their eyes to an all-night program whose characters were as familiar to them as the actors of sitcoms are to TV viewers today. But instead of punching a button on a remote control unit to animate their routine lives, these people used the catalytic touch of their imagination to bring the night to life.

Horses flew! Bears had tails! The sky was populated by dogs and cats, fish and fowl—creatures that the people knew by day and found reflected in the night.

They searched the heavens and found their heroes there too. Hercules, the Arnold Schwarzenegger of his time, and Perseus, who would, by all accounts, have been a match for James Bond (any one of them).

There was drama (murdered twins!) and beauty (ah, Venus) and a musical sound track (providing you like strings). There was even science fiction—giant crabs and a dragon that guarded the northern sky.

The show changed with the seasons and changed with the hour, and the more imaginative minds among these evening star watchers helped the less gifted by fitting the star-studded cast into stories and legends . . . until eyes drooped, heads followed, and it was time for sleep.

For thousands of years, evening viewers followed the night sky lineup, bringing stars to life. Then imaginative minds, being imaginative, began exploring other avenues to make legends come alive. They invented live programming—danced or sang or acted out the legends and drama they once had projected into the sky.

And people took their eyes away from the sky and watched what others created before them instead of what their minds could draw in the sky.

Then the imaginative minds invented the printed word and reading lamps, and lesser minds spent their evenings peering down at their laps—which was a problem because it left no place to put the buckets of popcorn, so books soon gave way to movie theaters.

Then came television, which is imagination's greatest creation—because it requires no imagination at all! And while people stared at the images dancing across the screen, they forgot that images danced overhead each night. Why, they never even noticed that the proliferation of lights (from TVs and porches and automobiles and office buildings and housing complexes) was erasing the fauna of the sky just as the light from the picture tube had erased them from people's minds.

The cancerous light increased, flooding the sky, washing away the Milky Way, crippling constellations, eclipsing lesser stars. Now, over urbanized parts of our country, an impenetrable curtain of light is drawn across the night sky. And the creatures of the night stand behind it. Beyond the reach of our imaginations. Even beyond the reach of our sight.

Unless! Unless you find some dark road beyond the glow of cities or towns. And pick some night when cold northwest winds fan the stars to a sharp-edged luster. And raise your face to the universe. And hold against the sky your handy Philips' Planisphere showing the principal stars visible for every hour of the year (useful in the middle latitudes).

"Let's see," I thought, turning south, turning the dial to the proper channel . . . er, setting. "The real bright one has to be Spica. Uh, no, that's a planet—probably Jupiter. O.K., then that one there. Has to be."

The star, a nice bright white one, was noncommittal.

I looked back at the map, searching for some other points of reference, and found what looked to be a pretty obvious five-star cluster, Corvus. According to the map, it would lie south and west of Spica.

And sure enough, there it was. It didn't exactly look like a raven, but, well, that's just my lack of imagination showing.

Bearings anchored, I turned my attention upon another bright star and consulted the chart for a name.

"Ah, Arcturus," I pronounced, pleased to meet a star that caught the fancy of poet Archibald MacLeish; Arcturus, which anchored the constellation Boötes. And between the megastars was a frail string of lesser kin. The constellation Virgo.

"Must be in recline," I concluded.

To the west was Leo. To the southeast, Libra. And just peeking over the horizon was a bright, blazing light that required no imagination—Venus. The Morning "Star."

The show was almost over for the night, it was true. But perhaps a new season featuring some classic reruns was just beginning.

Chasing Shadows

THE DEER paused at the edge of the trees, studying the open field before her. Not even the pain in her empty stomach could erase the lessons imparted by centuries, lessons of survival. Though her eyes had never beheld their living form, the shadows of timber wolves, mountain lions, and creatures more terrible than these still haunted her living dreams and lived in her ancestral memory.

In her mind, she could *see* the ring of eyes, moving like satellite embers around her. She could *hear* the crunch of snow under their feet as the ring of shadows tightened. She could *feel* the steamy breath explode from grinning jaws as the jaws closed over her—just before the coldest shadow would close over her mind.

Forever.

But for the present, the shadows *were* only in her mind. The meadow was empty, and it has been many years since timber wolves troubled the lives of deer in New Jersey; mountain lions, too. Other predators have replaced them, though now, as then, they are *nothing* compared to the Great Menace Starvation. The deer stepped away from the pines, into the open, leaving a trail of small dark holes in the snow. The snow was only a dusting beneath the pines, but in the field it lay thick and heavy. Although there was a crust, it was not strong enough to bear her weight. She broke through at every step.

Under the snow, there was grass—old grass, brown and

withered. The deer knew this. But the energy required to reach it would not justify the rewards. She could dig and forage on the thin winter grass until she starved.

The deer knew this too. It is the nature of deer to know when snow is too deep just as it is their nature to know where to bed down when the wind is bitter, or where the fresh young shoots will first appear in the spring (if they live to see the spring).

So the deer, an old doe who had seen many springs, made her way down the length of the field, inhaling the sweet warm smell of horses in a stable not far away, finding the break in the fence that surrounded the old orchard, moving toward the house with lights that glowed within and cast shadows without.

She became aware of other deer moving like starved gray spirits around the perimeter of the yard. A dozen, at least, were already foraging on assorted ornamental shrubs.

The truth was that there were too many deer (or, if you prefer, there were not enough shrubs). But altering the perspective doesn't alter the hard reality. There were too many deer, and there was not enough food, natural or otherwise, to sustain them all. The woodland browse was gone. During recent weeks, even the ornamental junipers right up against the house had been stripped of all that was edible and reachable. For what little remained, now, the foraging deer had to reach deep within the prickly maze.

In the house, a dog barked a challenge. The deer froze as shadows with ember eyes leaped into their minds. Several older deer ran a few short steps but stopped short of the trees. When the barking ceased, they moved quickly back to claim their place at the hedge.

The old doe did not linger. She knew the food was almost gone. She knew that the age that was in her made her a poor competitor. She knew a fool's errand when she saw one. Deer don't live as long as she had by accident.

She moved along the boxwood, keeping to the shadows, moving like a hunted thing. She was well away when she heard the bang of the screen door, the warning snort of startled deer, the excited barking of the dog, and the shouts of encouragement from the dog's owner. The shadows in her mind raised their heads and whined eagerly but fell back again as the barking became faint and distant.

From the trail that ran along the cyclone fence, she could hear the creatures that patrolled the long, dark river below her. In the middle of the river lay an island whose vegetation had not yet been stripped and where tender buds still clung to branches.

But the island was always guarded. Like mountain lions lying in ambush at a salt lick, like tireless wolves loping on an open plane, there was a predator here. A merciless creature that preyed upon her kind, and it lay between her and the food she needed to sustain her.

The risk was great. She had ventured to the island once, when she was a yearling, with the twin that was a sister. Both of them had reached the island. Only one survived the return. The risk was very great. But the alternatives were gone. From the break in the fence, she could hear the whine and growl of the creatures as they sped by. From deep within her mind, lupine shadows picked up their ears and trotted to the edge of her consciousness, whining a greeting to the predator of this age. Slowly, cautiously, the deer moved to the bank of the dark river and took shelter from the harsh gleam of predatory eyes behind a scrubby juniper.

The shadows in her mind leaned forward, crowding her thoughts, daunting her will with fear. But these were just the shadows of shadows compared to the *Great Dark Shadow* that stalked her from behind, cutting off any thought of retreat.

Once . . . twice, she came close to making her dash, but each time small groups of the bright-eyed predators crested the hill, forcing her to wait.

The ache inside her stomach and the sanctuary of trees drew her. The shadows coursing back and forth in her mind pressed her from behind. The lights that blazed and danced in her eyes confused and daunted her. The tension made her anxious, made her tremble, made it impossible to wait a moment longer. Danger or no, she had to go, she had to try she . . .

Leaped! And in her mind the pack of shadows leaped in

pursuit. The snow piled beside the dark river clutched at her legs, dragging her down. The ice that lay at the river's edge made her stumble, fall! But she was up again, and running again, running for the sanctuary of trees. Running for her life!

In the blazing lights, on the great river of asphalt, the shadows in her mind took on corporal form. They surrounded her. Closed in upon her. Their howling filled her mind. Through the fear that nearly blinded her, she could see nothing but the safety of the trees just ahead. Just ahead. Three leaps away. Two leaps. The safety of the trees. Just ahead . . .

She was on her side, reaching out with legs that could find no more footing on earth, so she stopped thrashing and lay still. Overhead, she could see stars gleaming through the steam that poured from the creature's jaws, and on her face, she could feel the creature's hot breath. But that was all she felt. The hunger was gone now; even the pain.

Dimly, she heard the crunch of snow under approaching feet. Vaguely she felt the shadows close in around her until they filled her mind. And then mercifully, mercifully, just when she thought she could endure no more, the howling of the pack became a whine, became a sigh, became an unearthly silence that lingered and spread . . .

Became nothing at all.

Dan Mutchler didn't feel much like a predator; in fact, he felt much more like a victim. He'd spent the entire morning tied up in a horrendous traffic jam—the result of too many cars, too much ice, and one too many jack-knifed tractor trailers. He'd missed an important meeting, gotten dumped on by a boss for being late, slugged it out in twenty miles of stop-and-go traffic in the homebound commute, and now he was looking at a dead deer and what was left of the front end of his car.

The timber wolf is gone over much of North America. The mountain lion, too. But these predators have been replaced by another predator, a top predator, one that preys upon all other creatures (including itself). That predator is the automobile.

Thus is balance maintained.

Hope

AFTER DINNER, while Jay made good his offer to do the dishes, we stepped out of the clubhouse and into the night. It was raining. But it didn't matter. It was late. That mattered even less.

We were dry and comfortable and warmed by several hours of good spirits. We had worked hard at the nets. We had taken enough fish for dinner. We had eaten our fill, talked our way into a fine mood, and we were content.

This is how it is to be at Hope.

Beyond the marshes and the distant trees, the glow of South Jersey towns smeared the sky with light. Overhead commuter jets crowded with homebound captains of industry snarled and whined. Both the lights and the jets served as reminders, if anyone cared to be reminded, that there was another world besides this one and it wasn't far away.

But that world, and all the trappings of that world, could not touch us, here, on this porch, of this old duck-hunting club, overlooking this Delaware Bay marsh. Here, we were immune because the demands of that world have no standing here. They stop where tires leave the pavement and fall into mud rut tracks, the tracks that lead to Hope.

"Great dinner, Bill," I said, complimenting the chef—who in that other life is a civil engineer.

"Thanks," he said. "Shad's a good fish."

"But not as good as striper [striped bass]," he added, trying to revive a conversation that had commanded much of the evening (but failing).

"The roe was great," said Tom, who prefers shad to striper and who, in that other world, is an attorney. It was Tom who had taken the glistening female shad, heavily laden with roe, out of our drift net that afternoon, lifting it high for appraising eyes and to whet appetites already sharpened by labor.

Hope, in case you are curious, is a real place, although you won't find it on a map. Hope is a club whose members gun in the fall, drop nets in the spring, crab pots in summer, and who, whenever they can, excuse themselves from that other world to find mooring in a Hope-filled one.

Metaphysical boundaries notwithstanding, Hope consists of five hundred acres of marsh and uplands, enough boats and blinds to serve, a clubhouse, a couple of outbuildings, and twelve members. Jay and Bill were members. Tom and I (and Jay's son and Bill's daughter, who were already sleeping the good sleep of exhausted children) were guests.

The clubhouse is nothing much to look at—a box on stilts that one might not call a shack out of politeness. Inside there is one large room that serves all functions. Flanking it are doors that lead to individual sleeping cells whose dimensions would induce claustrophobia in a monk.

The light fixtures bolted to the ceiling are gas. The stove that heats the room burns coal. Water is drawn from a pump and is brackish past the point of endurance.

The place looks like a shack, and it is a shack. But the roof is sound, the room is warm, and the smell—of coal and leather and gun oil and things that are cooked in butter—is not to be equaled. It is the kind of room that men like and that men feel comfortable in. It is a sanctuary and on either side of its door lies freedom.

No one has ever been turned away from Hope's door because their duck coat dripped brackish slush. No dog has ever been denied access because it was wet and muddy.

There is no room for formality at Hope. No opinion that cannot be expressed. No glass that is less than half full. No diets, no guilt, and no such thing as cholesterol.

"Cholesterol is not a problem so long as you remember to flush regularly," says Paul, who at seventy-eight is the club's patriarch and who, so saying, will direct his nearly half-empty tumbler toward the bottles on the counter and add "time for another flush."

There is no discrimination based upon race, religion, creed, sex, or age at Hope. And if most of those who come to Hope are men, it must mean that what Hope has to offer appeals mostly to men.

"People ask me whether my marriage suffers because I spend so much time here," observed Jay, who had finished the dishes and joined us on the porch. "But my wife says our marriage is so great because I spend time here."

Many women, I guess (because I am not a woman and cannot know), would not be surprised by the Spartan interior of the clubhouse. There are posted notices and paintings yellowed by age. There is a couch that sags and chairs that do not match and a table that looks as though it spent part of its life on a curb.

But there is one thing about Hope that some women might rightfully regard suspiciously. If not women, then wives, and if not wives in general then certainly my wife in particular. Despite the open-minded standards that apply to men and dogs, the clubhouse is neat and tidy. Not painfully so; just practically so.

Jackets are not thrown over chairs. Boots are not left in the center of the room. Gear is not stacked behind the door . . . or in a corner . . . or left on the counter . . .

Each man's belongings are placed, with care. Guns on the rack. Waders on the porch. Clothes hung on the hooks in each monk's cell, where all the other needs of life are stored— a flashlight that works, a pocketknife that cuts, shells chambered for that man's gun.

If the standards of Hope are simple, they balance realities that are hard. These realities include drift nets that must be hauled by hand until arms go numb; icy water, bottomless mud, and treacherous outboard motors that get you out but won't bring you back in.

At Hope life is dictated by the wind and the tide, sharpened by risk, and an incautious moment can throw life and death in the balance. One March night, several years ago, the doctor and two other club members clung to the hull of their overturned boat—and to life. They were not found until dawn, and only two lived to recount the experience today—which they sometimes do, which is their great privilege.

There are some, I'm sure, who will think that Hope is just a form of escapism—that people who draw nets across the tide and raise guns into the sky are substituting atavistic traditions for the realities of the modern world.

Well, the realities of the "modern world," the world I call the "other" world *are* real. They include meetings and flight schedules and state regulations and clients and court appearances and briefs. Time, in the "other world," is measured in minutes on somebody else's watch. Value is determined by market strategists and, when their estimates fail, by clearance sales.

These things of the other world are very real. But only because we accord them reality and only because the anxiety they induce is genuine.

But those realities are not as real as the realities of Hope. Where risk is more than missing your connection, time is measured by the tide, and the value of a thing is determined not by the esteem it holds for others but by the effort it takes to claim it and the satisfaction it brings to you.

It began to rain harder—but it still didn't matter, wouldn't, in fact, until it was time to haul net in the morning. It was later, too, and, sadly, this had begun to matter. First Tom said goodnight and disappeared, then Bill. Jay and I stood for a time, listening to the night sounds of marsh and the drum of rain on a roof that did not leak. In time, we followed the others and retired to the bunks, in the cells, where all the things a man might need are found.

Save one.

Across the marsh and beyond the distant wall of trees, New Jersey residents had put the things of their world aside and traded their hopes for dreams. But here, at Hope, a select few were sleeping the uncomplicated sleep of those who have already reached their dreams—if only for a little while.

Dear Floyd

I'M SORRY this letter is late. I'd planned on coming to visit you at the hospital yesterday afternoon. Then I got the call from your son, Bob, at work. He told me the news.

Nice fellah, Bob. You have a father's right to be proud. I guess I should say "had," shouldn't I? That's going to take some getting used to. I'll probably slip up now and again in this letter. I hope that's all right.

I'm at Deer Path Farm, and it's pretty early even by bird-watching standards. The cold front that cleared the night you died went on through. The wind dropped off just after midnight. The high must be right on top of us.

I think it was the quiet that woke me, but it could have been the moon coming in through the window. It's full now. Anyway, I couldn't go back to sleep. I just lay there, listening to the great-horned owls, thinking and remembering.

It came to me after a while that what I was doing was thinking a letter. And so I decided to get up and set it down on paper. Let's see what a memory looks like, huh?

So far, it looks pretty jumbled and disorganized, doesn't it? I can't seem to find all the great lines and high-born phrases that I had just an hour ago. I'm not sure, now, what it was that I wanted to say or how to go about saying it. I'm not sure whether I'm trying to tell a story or write a eulogy or just say "thank you for everything."

It feels like someone kicked the bottom out of the world,

and I'm having trouble taking stock because things are still in the process of falling.

One thing that I really wanted to say is that I think you were a great man. I bet you'll get a kick out of that. I had to change my notion of what a great man was in order to fit you in, the notion they teach you at school. But that's O.K. The notion was wrong and needed changing.

When you think of greatness, you think of people like Thomas Jefferson, Charles Lindbergh, and Bruce Springsteen. Next to them, I guess that a retired teamster from Nutley, New Jersey, named Wolfarth, who raised his family, paid his bills on time, and scraped and saved to buy a corner of the world in Warren County is a funny candidate for greatness. But I don't think you'll get any arguments from any of the people who knew you.

What was it like being a bird watcher fifty years ago? Or did you call yourselves bird lovers then (or was that something people called you?).

See, there are still lots of questions that I need to ask. That was the basis of our partnership. I asked the questions, and you had the answers.

With sixty million people throwing seed to the birds these days, society has gotten a little bit more relaxed about the subject of birding. I don't feel that I have to defend my manhood every time I pick up a pair of binoculars and head for the local woodlot.

But I'll bet that fifty years ago a freight hauler who planned his runs to catch the broad-winged hawk flights at Montclair or scheduled his pick ups to search for Iceland gulls in the Hackensack Meadows on his lunch hour was quite an anomaly.

Boy, you were a good field I.D. man, one of the best hawk and gull people I've ever seen—and I've seen almost all of them now.

Do you remember our first trip to Newburyport, Massachusetts? The first-winter black-headed gull? Six quadrillion Bonaparte's gulls sleeping in a mound a quarter of a mile away, and you say:

"Yes, sir. Got a black-headed."

Six of us studied that bird for twenty minutes, hemming and hawing. Then the thing brings up its head, and sure enough, the critter's got a red bill.

I asked you how you knew, and you said, "Bigger bird. More bulk. Stands out."

Yeah, the way a softball tucked in a pile of hardballs at the left-field wall stands out from home plate.

I wonder if Bruce Springsteen could have picked out a black-headed gull at that distance. I wonder how many birds Jefferson had on his New Jersey list, or whether Lindbergh ever birded with Charles Urner in the Elizabeth Meadows.

If I've heard it once, I've heard it a hundred times, the story about your mew gull. I can just see it. Half the high-muck-a-mucks of North American birding standing shoulder to shoulder on the seawall, all searching for some lipstick-colored gull from Siberia—the bird that Roger Tory Peterson called "the bird of the century"—and you shout, "Mew gull!"

Talk about guts! If the bird had headed out of the harbor, you would have been a royal goat. But no, the bird comes in like a chickadee to St. Francis' beckoning hand and plops down in front of two hundred spotting scopes.

Incidentally, I was talking to Roger the other day. He asked me to give you his regards. He wanted me to tell you how much he enjoyed all your letters.

Did I ever tell you how much I appreciated the notes you used to leave on my windshield while I was doing those spring migration counts up on the ridge? I never kept them, but I remember them.

"No flight, right? Colder than a necromancer's mammary gland. Mercury so high it's looking down on Gasherbum II. Nothing on top but one frozen Downy Woodpecker. Am I right? Stop by for a beer buddy. Fill me in on the count. O.K.?"

It kind of reminded me of the tooth fairy in a way. I'd leave a VW bug, the color of a back molar, tucked below the ridge. Later, I'd reach my hand under the windshield wiper and close my fist around a nickel's worth of wisdom. One nickel every day. It added up.

The great-horned owls are calling again. Can you hear them? The female's on eggs in the spruce grove behind the house. They were pretty rambunctious in February, but they've been quiet since the female started incubating. They usually only call near dawn, now.

Maybe the moon's making them vocal. Maybe the stillness is making them uneasy.

I never got to show you the farm, did I? I never got a chance to go up on the ridge with you last fall (too busy saving the environment, as we say in the trade).

It's going to take a while to come up with an accounting of what's been lost. I touch the subject cautiously, the way you explore the hole in your tooth when the dentist leaves the room.

I guess when people mention your name now they'll be using the same reverent tones that people use when they recall the likes of Charles Urner and Lee Edwards and Maurice Broun—all of the ornithological greats. But, then, so were you. One of the greatest. And the one who took it upon himself to . . .

Huh. A cardinal just started to sing. That's pretty weird. I've heard them sing at night under a full moon later in the breeding season, but they just started their dawn chorus a week ago and . . .

Oh, I see.

Listen, I've got to close. If I don't get off on time, I get killed in the commuter traffic on Route 78. But listen, some of the guys are planning something for you this fall—when the broad-winged hawks move through—a sort of ceremony. And another thing. I still have your copy of Stone's *Bird Studies at Old Cape May*.

Do you mind if I hold onto it a while longer?

Best regards, always,
Pete

P.S.   I went up to the ridge yesterday afternoon to see if anything was moving. I counted five red-tailed hawks, one Cooper's hawk, and an immature bald eagle.

P.P.S.   Listen, if you run into Maurice Broun, tell him I said "Hi!"

Ice Out

THERE ARE small signs of spring that I search for. I need them to keep my faith alive. I need them for the assurance they bring. Each is a victory against winter, and they mount, these vernal victories, day by day, one atop the other until the sheer weight of them flips the earth on its axis . . . and suddenly, I find myself searching for lingering signs of winter instead.

There are *many* signs, in *many* places—pintails that gather on the sheltered banks of water courses . . . honeybees that cast their dead upon the snow . . . rivers of crows that flow north along the flanks of the Appalachians . . . coltsfoot that blooms with its back to a ridge and its face to the sun.

But among all these little skirmishes, there is, to my mind, one deciding victory—a long campaign fought between two seasons whose termination marks the end of one season and the beginning of another. There is even a name for it. It is called "ice out"—the day that winter's lock is picked and ponds become ponds; rivers flow like rivers again.

Here, in New Jersey, "ice out" is an obscure term. The state straddles the Mason-Dixon Line and lies at the limit of winter's reach. It's almost as if the season advances to the terminal moraine of the Laurentide Ice Sheet (that great winter victory of ten thousand years ago) and gets cold feet. Sometimes New Jersey's larger lakes don't freeze until January. There have even been years, in South Jersey and along the shore, when they have not frozen at all.

But farther north, ice out is a very real and very significant event. It is something you will hear spoken of in the post office, the dry goods store, and in the diner, over coffee, where the town worthies gather to chew the cusp of events.

"D'ja hear Deer Lake's open? Ice out's kinda early this year, don't ya think?"

"Do tell. Funny. Thought spring was runnin' late. Must be me running late. Top me up would ya please, Betty, then I guess I gotta run."

In Fairbanks, Alaska, breakup is a veritable pageant. There's even a lottery associated with the event. Can you guess the day, hour, and minute that the Nanana River breaks up? The monetary prize is substantial—so much so that a watchful eye is kept for any dynamiters who might be tempted to try to nudge the natural process along.

Incidentally, "breakup," strictly speaking, is used in reference to rivers. "Ice out" applies to lakes—but it all comes down to the same thing. Winter looses its grip, and water slips through its icy fingers.

I guess I like ice out because it falls within the natural rhythm of change. It is an event in harmony with the season, and spring plays a different tune every year. Sometimes the season runs early, and lakes are free in February. Sometimes the season runs late, and lakes remain in their icy sheaths until the downside of March. If this seems capricious, this flexible freeze, well, spring *is* capricious. And as a measure of spring, ice out is more accurate than a silly date stamped on a calendar and more attuned to reality than the prognosticating powers professed by some sleep-drugged Pennsylvania ground hog.

I guess I like ice out, too, because it unfolds gradually, give and take. It gains a few days, then the winds turn northerly, and it loses a week. Watching the ice retreat each spring taught me patience and taught me faith. Caution, too! There is a point where ice stops being supportive, and reckless boys, like reckless dynamiters, may help the natural process along.

Sunlight is the great enemy of ice. The ice tries to defend itself by reflecting the light back, but it can do nothing about the heat energy trapped in the surrounding air or the surrounding banks. And like nylon in the sun, the ice weakens and rots. Dark objects lying on the surface or trapped in the ice absorb the radiant energy and burn free of the imprisoning walls. The dark earth along the northern lakeshore heats quickly, and the ice loses its grip—beginning the long, slow retreat that will end, days later, in the shadows of the far shore.

Wind helps the melting process. So does rain or the force of spring floods gushing from feeder streams. But it is the sun that moves the seasons.

There are setbacks, of course. At night the temperatures fall, and morning may find a thin, brittle layer of ice covering the lake again. Winter may rally and bury the region in an ocean of arctic air or blanket the lake in a protecting buffer of snow. But the outcome is inevitable. For forty-two years, I've never known spring to lose out. And though I know how the story ends, I love to follow the nuances of each and every revisionary plot.

Spring doesn't wait until total victory before colonizing its gains. Even before a body of water is properly de-iced— even before ice out progresses much beyond the point of dark open leads along the sunny shore—waterfowl arrive. In New Jersey, flocks of common merganser reach the Delaware River in late January. And as I sat, writing this piece, a prospecting pair of Canada geese came in and checked the small (and still frozen) farm pond across the street.

But there is a rather special duck that is, to me, symbolic of ice out—and spring. It is a freshwater duck (so not one likely to be found toughing out winter along the coast). And this bird does not nest in New Jersey. Home for this colorful diving duck lies in the forested lakes and bogs of Canada and a handful of far northern states.

The bird's name is the ring-necked duck and, like spring, it is transitory. Ring-necked ducks appear when open water appears. They depart before the bloodroot pokes its blossoms through the leaves cast by another season. On reservoirs and large, open lakes, rafts of several hundred birds may be found during March. But even the most humble pond will host a few birds in the course of a spring—small flocks that will put in for an hour or two and then depart.

It's a handsome duck, shy and intolerant of observers. It is also somewhat misnamed. The pale, copper-colored ring encircling the iridescent neck of males is almost impossible to see. As names go, "ring-billed" duck would have served the bird better. But I have actually seen, yes, really *seen* the ring on the neck of the ring-necked duck—seen it once. It happened many springs ago on the ponds behind my parents' house. It happened on a spring morning that was more winter than spring, and it was, appropriately enough, the first time I had ever set eyes on the bird.

The ice had retreated halfway across the pond, but the edge was invisible through the snow that fell hissing into the water. The shadow flock with the whistling wings emerged from the gray curtain, circled once, and retreated behind the curtain. The muffled splash of its landing barely reached the shore.

The birds took their time approaching the cove. The sheltered place would keep them out of the wind, but it would find them disturbingly close to the wall of trees. As the distance fell away, the flock became six individual birds, then four male and two female diving ducks, and finally, six ring-necked ducks.

Their heads were fully erect, straining to detect whatever menace lurked along the shore. From a distance that could be measured in mere feet, the subtle ring around the neck of each male bird was plain to see. I didn't need to see the ring to identify the birds, but for some odd reason, it's important to see the mark that is the namesake of a bird to feel comfortable with an identification.

The birds remained as long as I did, which was as long as I could bear the cold and the cramp in my legs. They disappeared between the time I stood and the time I turned to leave.

I see ring-necked ducks every year, and I will search for them again this year—a black and white cluster of ducks halfway across a half-frozen lake. And I will smile because in my mind I will recall those six birds that I met at the edge of winter one day. And because I will know that the next step I take will carry me into spring.

Onion Snow

SHE WAS standing behind the sliding glass door that opened onto the wooded ridge. She was looking at the birds coming to the feeder, and she was looking at the snow. I poured a cup of coffee and joined her.

"Where's Linder?" Debbie asked, betraying, at once, the practical interest of a host and her Down East roots.

"Still struggling with the new day," I confided, smiling. Linda, my wife, is a slow starter on cold mornings.

Debbie smiled too, but her eyes and her thoughts remained on the snow.

"This is sort of unexpected," I said, meaning the snow.

"It's an onion snow," she returned. "It means nothing."

There was silence for a time, and that was time enough to let a wordsmith savor the taste and texture of a fresh new phrase. Some people collect coins. Some collect stamps. I collect words and terms, and the one I'd just been handed was a gem.

"Is that an expression they use in Maine?" I wanted to know. "Onion snow," I added, because the minds of nature writers and the minds of engineers do not necessarily drift in the same direction.

"No," Debbie replied. "It's something I picked up from the gentlemen farmers who lived next door. Or maybe I got it from Betty," she amended. Betty was Debbie's old housekeeper, a Hunterdon County native and a person who didn't mind getting her hands in dirt whether it lay inside a house or out.

"It's a gardener's expression," Tom, Debbie's husband, said, stepping up to the coffee maker and into the conversation. "It's a snow that falls too late in the season to affect spring growth."

"Onion snow," I thought, immersing myself in the term. "I think I'll take a walk before breakfast," I announced.

I took the path behind the stable, across the field flanked by pines and up the old logging road. The flakes were thick and fluffy. They floated more than fell and covered the trunks of trees.

Beneath the new coating, in protected hollows, the old snow lay deep. It was crusty on top and crunchy underfoot. There had been a lot of snow during the winter, and much had lingered.

But along sunny banks and sloping hillsides, the onion snow fell upon fresh-turned earth. It put a sparkle on wild daffodils and threw a showy robe over the clumps of onion grass poking up through last year's growth.

"Onion snow."

I guess I've known onion snows all my life. But until offered the catalytic framework of Debbie's expression, I'd never consciously noticed that April snows are different from other snows—from November snows or March snows—though clearly they are. And in case you think that the things that distinguish onion snows from other snows are just the machinations of a writer's mind, you should know that other creatures (besides gardeners) recognize the difference too.

Take birds. Debbie's feeders were active. Goldfinches and house finches claimed the high ground. Juncos and white-throated sparrows foraged below.

But the feeding was leisurely, orderly. Squabbles were few, and feeder perches sometimes went wanting. This is how birds behave during an onion snow.

A snowfall in December is different. It puts ferocity into the feeding behavior of birds. Squabbles are the rule, and perches are fought for as if life and death hang in the balance (and they do).

Debbie's birds, by their actions, were saying precisely what Debbie had said. "It's an onion snow. It means nothing." No bitter cold to follow. No heat-leaching winds. No icy encasement over the food that birds need to survive.

Onion snow. It's an event that even creatures that lead lives as precarious as birds can laugh at—sing at, too! Because while an onion snow might block the sun for a time, it can't turn back the clock. Onion snow falls on cardinals who throw back their heads and warble, juncos that trill, and white-throated sparrows that whistle their phonetic lament to "Oh Sweet Canada, Canada Canada."

Onion snows fall upon spring, and spring only moves in one direction. It moves toward summer.

The road got steeper. The old snow lay deeper. My breaths grew shorter, and suddenly, I was overdressed. First, gloves were shucked. Then the hat was pocketed. Before the road topped the hill, I was out of my jacket too, and the flakes fusing to my sweater only added to the warmth.

An onion snow is a warm snow, and though you may sneer at the thought, it makes it no less so. Skiers understand this, and backpackers, and kids who shovel driveways, too.

In December, snow is hard and prickly. It stings faces and creeps down collars and makes a body yearn for a merry blaze in a brightly lit room.

In March, snow is sodden and heavy and wraps itself around you like a cold, wet cat. It soaks garments and makes you think fondly of package tours to tropical places.

But an onion snow is warm, and it is soft. It closes over garments without melting, and it falls on a face like a kiss.

There is something else about an onion snow that is compelling, maybe alluring. There is a feel to onion snow, an aura that is akin to innocence—but of course it is much too late for innocence. You know it. The season knows it. There is no use kidding about it.

It is not innocence. So it must be an apology. And it seems to me that the onion snow strives to make amends

for whatever hardships might have fallen before. The onion snow is like the child who has broken the vase and offers a fistful of flowers. Onion snow is like the divorced spouse you meet for lunch who says, "There were good times too; it wasn't so bad."

The onion snow says, "See, I am making the world beautiful for you." And it is so.

The onion snow says, "Look. See where the deer bed down. *There.* The dark ovals in the snow. They fled when they heard us coming. You would not know they were there but for me."

And this too is so.

The onion snow says, "*There!* The cuttings atop the snow. A squirrel fed here. You would have missed that. And *there!* The tracks of rabbits. The two of them. See how they chased. See how they played. See all the things I can show you."

Yes and yes again. It is just as the onion snow says.

And then the onion snow says, "All the cold and ice that you remember. The bitter winds. The long, dark nights. The chill that could not be shaken. That was a mistake. That is not how I am. This," the onion snow says, "is how I really am."

And this too is true. But it is only true in April, in the time of the onion snow.

The road was heading down now, heading back. The snow was not so heavy, and the sky not so gray. It would not be long before the sun burned through and not much longer before the snow, both the old and the new, was gone.

"Will you miss me?" the onion snow wanted to know.

The house hove into view. Debbie and Amy and now Linda were framed behind the glass. I made the door, stepped across the threshold into the mudroom, and stomped my feet, sending snow flying.

Outside it snowed until it stopped. It remained until it melted. And in Debbie's garden, beneath a warm, spring sun, the onions flourished.

For the Span of a Firefly's Light

THE DISHES were washed and dried. The urgent tasks that clog a weekend docket had been scratched off the list (or forgotten until next week).

"It's still light," I observed. "Want to sit outside?"

"You bet," Linda, my eternal bride, replied. "You bet," the archetypal Western affirmation. It's a short term for a part of the country that measures distance by the horizon, but one that can cover any query from "Hot, ain't it?" to "Do you want salsa on your eggs?"

"You bet."

If words had a smell, your nose would tingle with the scent of sage. If you could taste a term, it would lie flinty and dry on the tongue. In the hot mugginess of a New Jersey summer evening, one filled with the hum of cicadas, the laconic syllables sounded mildly incongruous, slightly out of place. I tried to suppress a grin and failed.

"Look," Linda said, gathering my attention and focusing it on the shrubbery nearby. "Fireflies!"

Sure enough, in the darker places where the bushes were already cemented by shadow, the first fireflies of the evening were tuning up. Here and there, a yellow spark would flicker and fade. Soon the backyard would be filled with them.

"Do you remember how you used to catch them and put them in bottles when you were a kid," I remarked, casually.

There was silence for a time.

"We didn't have fireflies in California," Linda replied. "Or Alberta," she added to fill the silence that was putting distance between us.

I don't think I could have been more surprised if she had confessed that "out West, people didn't celebrate the Fourth of July or eat popsicles or play inningless baseball until it was too dark to see a pop fly."

No fireflies! I tried to imagine a childhood without fireflies, and my mind recoiled from the thought.

"Are you sure?" I said, turning to confront the truth of it in Linda's face.

"You bet," she replied, backing up her assurance with an affirmative nod.

"You mean to tell me that you grew up and never saw a firefly?"

"Too true," she admitted. "The closest I ever came to fireflies was the 'Pirates of the Caribbean' exhibit at Disneyland."

The disclosure made me shudder and came close to bankrupting the natural treasures of the American West in my mind. Fireflies (to my mind) are an absolutely integral part of childhood. Why, a backyard without fireflies would be like a sky with all the stars erased from it. It was unthinkable!

It is pretty clear (even to adults) that fireflies are magical creatures—among the last such creatures on earth. Science has methodically killed off the rest by discovering the secrets behind the magic and turning magical creatures into "ordinary phenomena." Knowledge, even insight, is fatal to anything magical.

But fireflies continue to confound science. How these transistor-sized beetles can produce cold light with an energy efficiency approaching 100 percent (while your basic incandescent lamp runs at about 10 percent efficiency) is a mystery—is *magic!*

As it is, I already know more about fireflies than I care to: inconsequential things like what species are found in New Jersey, how long they live as adults. I would pass this stuff on to you, but peddling this brand of information only serves to compromise what little magic is left on earth. It comes pretty close to science or treason, and I relish neither.

If I'm going to dwell on fireflies at all, I'm more inclined to discuss matters of consequence (like how to go about catching them). Without much effort, I can still recall the best yards in my old neighborhood and a dozen places where fireflies were so thick you were afraid to inhale—places where three or four good firefly catchers could fill a quart-sized milk bottle before fathers would step onto porches and whistle the kid-specific notes that sent neighborhood youngsters sprinting for home.

Milk bottles worked better than Coke bottles. The mouths were wider. If you used a Coke bottle, you had to pinch the insect with your fingers (and that usually hurt it some). With a milk bottle, you could just palm the insects in a fist and drop them in like incandescent jelly beans.

Experienced firefly catchers prefer milk bottles four to one.

Another good thing about milk bottles was that later, when you went to bed, it was easier to get the fireflies out. After a goodnight, you could almost fill a bedroom with silent yellow explosions, and constellations would form on the ceiling that had no names except the ones that you gave them.

I have become mortally afraid that the secret of firefly light is not long for this world. The probings of science are relentless, and recent discoveries in the field of superconductivity make me nervous.

When the secret is out, there will be one less magical creature left on earth. And the world will be a poorer place for it.

The cicadas had shut down for the night. The last notes of a robin's evening song ended abruptly. On the hillside, a whip-poor-will began to assert itself.

The fireflies followed the lengthening shadows into the yard, flowing from the dark places in waves that pulsed. Some hugged the ground. Others spiraled skyward. Most flashed yellow or white, but here and there, one would glow with a blue-green light.

Linda and I braved the dew-laden grass to move closer to the action, and at our feet, mating pairs made the grass tremble with sparks. Overhead, constellations came and went with secondhand regularity.

There was a part of me that listened for the sound of a whistle that would call me home for the night. But it never came. All of the adults, it seemed, had disappeared.

"Try and catch one," I invited.

"You'll laugh," she said, laughing.

"Go ahead," I coaxed. "I'm doing a study. I want to see whether catching fireflies is innate or learned behavior. Go on. Give it a try."

Clint Eastwood never turned his back on a challenge, and neither does Linda.

Without another word, this person—whose childhood I only know as the memories told by others, whose childhood lay a continent and two decades away—edged into the yard. Leaning forward, weight balanced on the balls of her feet, her legs spaced for balance, she studied the targets around her.

Maybe there aren't any fireflies in California, but it was clear that this person had caught a butterfly or two in her time and snagged more than her share of wind-blown cotton grass tufts.

Linda ignored the insects already in the grass. No challenge there. She closed in on a group of males flashing in a bright but desultory fashion—a typical amateur's mistake.

Any seven-year-old from New Jersey can tell you that you're better off picking the quick flashers or the double-flashers. Linda's two-handed grab came up empty.

Not bad form, I mused. Hotdoggers try to one-hand 'em but usually succeed only in batting the insect to the ground. I might have guessed that anyone who used to teach mountaineering skills wouldn't be cocky enough to risk a one-handed grab.

Linda tried again, and missed again.

"This isn't like trying to catch trout with your hands is it?" she challenged.

"No," I assured, surveying the insects around me, selecting one that was firing in fast, regular bursts, picking him off.

"Here," I said, displaying my prize with an open hand.

"It's just like riding a bicycle," I added apologetically.

Linda accepted the evidence on face value and re-doubled her efforts.

"Pick out a quick flasher," I coached.

"No fair giving me any help," she declared. But she also changed her tactics.

I saw the firefly she wanted almost as soon as she did. I saw the way her steps quickened with purpose, saw how her eyes grew fixed like a lioness on the hunt.

I watched how she slowed to a stalk as she and the magical creature drew near; how her raised hands tensed, elbows cocked and ready.

I watched how skillfully she crowded her target against the hedge, how the hands darted forward, how the stars overhead held their breaths, and how the flickering light disappeared.

And when Linda turned, with eyes that gleamed with triumph and a prize to show me clasped in her hands, I saw, for the span of a firefly's light, a glimpse of the little girl whose childhood I know only as the memory of others.

Such is the magic of fireflies.

The Perfect Table

"SEE IF YOU can pick out the right one," Linda challenged. "O.K.," I said, releasing her hand and stepping into the showroom, a labyrinth filled with chairs and tables and sofas and, somewhere in hiding, one or two salespeople. Linda fell a step behind, anxious but confident too; confident that the table she had discovered here was perfect beyond question or doubt; confident that our tastes were so wonderfully matched that I could not help but agree.

And I did see it, almost instantly, across a sea of bloated lounge chairs, Byzantine lamps, and couches modeled after Fort Apache—the perfect dining room table.

"That one," I said, pointing, and I did not need to see the smile or the happy nod to know I was right. Even from across the room, even without a halo over it, you could tell that this was the one.

It was a drop-leaf table of Shaker lines, long and uncommonly narrow. I think I've heard these things referred to as "harvest tables," but that may be wrong, and frankly I don't much care. What's in a name? Leaves down, it stood like a ballerina in repose; leaves flared, it brought to mind the effortless flight of seabirds. The wood was dark and lustrous, the grain almost fathomless in its complexity. But I don't buy cars or tables for their color. I wanted to kick the tires and slam the door, lift the leaf and check out the supports.

I lifted one of the leaves, marveling at the great weight of it. I studied the construction, appreciating the careful fittings and joints. "Solid," I concluded, no question about it.

The design was a marvel of simplicity, but the artist who crafted it had gambled the farm on two adornments. The corners were cut on a bias. On a lesser table, this might have compromised the Shaker simplicity, but on this table, all it did was shake some of the austerity from it. The other adornment was riskier—an inset border that differed from the balance of the tabletop by a shade or two. It could have been garish; it could have put the kibosh on the whole affair. But it did not. The border was so subtle that, without the proper light or a pure heart, it was almost invisible. It set the table off, beautifully.

"So," I thought. "The table has a halo after all. It's built right into the wood."

In a word, the table was perfect. *Perfect!* I could easily envision Socrates, standing at the far end, nodding his head, mumbling approval, into his beard.

"Ummm, yes. Very close to the Ideal, this one. Very close, indeed, young man."

Perfect! Even *more* than perfect; why, this most perfect of tables was even discounted. Tableness at bargain basement rates.

"Look," I said, pointing to the descriptive tag and the printed figure slashed by a pen and written over. "They've even knocked it down." It all seemed too good to be true.

And it was. The table had a fatal flaw, horns within the halo. This table, the tag advised, was "mahogany."

You know about the destruction of the tropical rain forests, I guess, and growing world concern. Whole organizations have sprung up, making it the focus of their fear, and even Hollywood has made a fetish of rain forest protection (so it *must* be approaching the level of a household concern).

Sixty percent of the richest woodlands in the New World has already been destroyed; the rest is disappearing. When it's gone, a virtual Eden of plants and animals will go with it, including many North American birds that depend upon the forests of Central and South America during our winter.

Mahogany, one of the prized "cabinet woods," is a rain forest tree. Towering above the understory, these solitary giants stand one to an acre, and the felling and removing of just one assures the destruction of much that stands around it. But the quality of the wood, and the willingness of people to pay exorbitant prices to possess such quality, makes the logging and destruction profitable.

Logging for timber is not, of course, the only reason that rain forests all over the world are being destroyed. But it is a major factor, and by buying this table, in this New Jersey furniture showroom, Linda and I would be aiding and abetting the destruction of the rain forests. What's more, and unlike many who might step into this showroom, we knew it.

"It's mahogany," I said, evenly, trying not to impart by inflection any sign of judgment.

My observation didn't register at first, but then I saw Linda's eyes widen with understanding, and darken with loss. Then something else happened to the eyes. They narrowed and hardened. Whatever thoughts lay behind those hooded eyes were shielded from me. But I could guess their nature because the same thoughts were bubbling up in my own mind. They came in a blind rush, legions of angry objections, and they came armed for battle.

"So what?" the legions screamed. "So it's mahogany. Millions of acres of rain forest and you're worried about a couple of planks lopped off one lousy tree. Drop in the bucket.

"And what difference does it really make," the legions reasoned. "The tree's already cut. If you don't buy it, somebody else will. Might as well be you, right?"

"Might as well be me," I repeated in my mind.

"And another thing," the legions continued, sensing my weakness, pressing their advantage. "What the heck, right?" Mahogany, maple, hickory, pine. You want an omelet, you gotta break eggs; you want a table made of wood, you gotta cut down a tree. Them's the facts, right?"

I couldn't fault the logic. Looking toward the other end of the table, I invited an expert's opinion. Socrates was still standing there. The old philosopher was drumming his lips with his fingers, studying my moral dilemma with a detached professional air.

Standing next to him was another figure, slighter, but similarly garbed. His eyes were studying me the way a woodsman takes the measure of a tree he means to fell. His mouth was set and grim, and the lantern he carried in his hand made the table that lay between us glow.

"Look," I said to them, "I do socially redeemable things for a living. You know. Protect wetlands, save endangered species, educate the public about the need to protect critical habitat. But I really want this table."

"That's right," the supporting legions sang in chorus. "That's right."

The Master of Reason stopped playing with his lips. His eyes widened to childlike proportions, and he nodded his understanding. His companion merely glowered.

"I'm an environmentalist," I insisted. "I don't eat burgers at this fast-food joint because it uses styrofoam; I'm boycotting another because they buy their beef from the tropics. I recycle, and I give money to a swarm of conservation groups."

"That's right," the chorus intoned. "That's right."

"It's right," I shouted. "It's perfect. It's what we want. If anyone asks, we can say we inherited it. We can just say we didn't know.

"It's . . . perfect," I concluded lamely.

Socrates merely shrugged, but his companion smiled, a grim smile that moved only the corners of his mouth.

"Perfect," he said in mocking mimicry, and then he placed his lamp on the table. The lamp made the dead wood glow with life—all except for the center. The light from that lamp showed the flaw that no words or veneer could hide. At the very heart of it, the table was rotten, morally tainted. We could ignore it. We could sidestep it. We could lie about it. But we couldn't change it.

"We can't buy it," I heard Linda say. I'd forgotten her in the midst of the argument, but I looked at her now. She was sad but resigned, and her eyes were clear again.

"No," I agreed. "We can't." And we didn't. We left the showroom and the table behind. It's *still* there, that nearly perfect table with the halo veneer and the rottenness at the core, there for the taking.

If you want it.

Why Lawns?

A SACRED COW is about to be gored here—fodder for thought. Fair warning! If your lawn is your life, if you yearn for the smell of grass clippings, if you live for the throb of a John Deere riding mower between your legs, *pass this essay by.*

Like most people, I never thought much about lawns as I was growing up, certainly never questioned their existence. As one cut from the suburban block, I considered lawns to be a simple fact of life. They defined our property and the world as we knew it.

I cut the lawn; therefore, I live (here).

Well, I'm older now. Not particularly smarter but wiser— engendered with that deep, deep wisdom that many a wasted Saturday instills in a person. And one Saturday not long ago, I cut a swath right to the heart of the matter. I asked the question that sent the foundation of my suburban world tumbling on its axis. I pose it to you now.

Why lawns? *Why* must houses be surrounded by a vegetative cover that cannot possibly exist in nature? Where was it ever decreed that human dwellings must sit in a little green puddle whose purpose is to lie flat and look green?

Look. This is the plain truth. Here we are, you and me, living in a nice, temperate climate, blessed with changing seasons, adequate rainfall, fertile soils, and vegetative diversity. Left to their own devices, all the nice, coddled suburban lawns would cheerfully go through several stages of succession and in a hundred years or so would revert to nice mature climax forest.

In our dining room, there is an oil painting done in the style of the Hudson River School. Its principal subjects are two Native Americans meeting in the forest. Two things about the painting are noteworthy. First, the figures are shaking hands, which as greetings go, was not common practice among Native Americans.

Maybe the painter was inspired by Thomas Hobbes. Maybe the painter just didn't know much about American Indian culture.

The other thing, the striking thing about the painting, is the setting. Surrounding the glen are trees the likes of which I have never seen. Massive trees! Trees that simply dwarf the figures in the glen. They aren't imaginary trees, either. Nobody could imagine a forest this grand. Whoever the artist was, he had actually seen the great eastern forests before they were cut and burned in the advance of pioneer farmers.

And nobody has seen such forests since.

Wonderful things, woodlands. You don't have to seed them. You don't have to water them. You don't have to trim them, fertilize them, marinate them in toxins, or even care about them. Over most of North America, forests just happen. So why not let them?

Oh, I can hear the gears of the grass lobby turning. "Prairie! What about prairie? Grasslands are just as natural as forests." And a lawn is nothing but a prairie with a crew cut, right?

Well, no, it's not. A prairie is a complex mix of plants whose interrelationships are hardly less complex than DNA. A lawn is just grass, one species, and this sort of monoculture is an anathema to nature.

A lawn, to nature's way of looking at things, is just plain boring. That's why nature works overtime trying to spice things up—with dandelions, crab grass, and seedlings. (And that is why a whole lawn care industry has developed and millions of dollars are spent every year trying to stop nature from doing its job.)

I repeat: *Why lawns?* Why *can't* houses be surrounded by trees? Why is it that whenever a developer goes into a woodland, the first priority becomes making the future site of "Old Hickory Estates" or "Maple Slough Condominiums" resemble Carthage after the third Punic War? Why can't developers just surreptitiously drop in the units and leave the woods intact?

Attention prospective homeowners. Consider the considerable advantages of having a forest. Consider first the privacy. You get home from a hard day at work. You want to just shed your button-down oxford and have a beer in the privacy of your backyard without your neighbor hanging over the fence, telling you you're putting on weight. Well, with a forest fortress surrounding your suburban castle, you can.

You say you don't want to look at the remains of the 1968 Mustang convertible that your neighbor's son started taking down in the driveway in 1989. Well, relax. Veiled behind a curtain of trees, you can't.

Forests are cool, nice and cool in the summer—about ten degrees cooler under the canopy than areas subjected to the direct rays of the sun. Forests are quiet too. A nice woodland border serves as a buffer against boisterous parties or jam sessions that get out of hand. In winter, when you might like to have a little more cheap solar radiation, the canopy of deciduous woodlands obliges. It falls to earth, letting sunlight in.

All right, you got me. Having a forest means having to clean out the gutters once a fall. You're telling me you'd rather cut grass every weekend?

Try to picture it. There you are, Saturday afternoon, reclining on your patio. Cold drink in one hand, a good book in the other, and not a mower to be heard. Downtown, the bank thermometer reads 95 degrees Fahrenheit. Your thermometer reads 83. Your neighbor hails through a break in the trees.

"Hello, John. How's it going?"

"Just fine, Phil. Real fine."

"Forest looks terrif this year. Doing anything different?"

"Nope. Not a thing."

Literally, not a thing. No raking (what's the sense of raking a forest?). No cutting the understory (it's part of the natural ambiance, part of what makes a forest a forest).

Dead trees? Well, what about them? Dead trees are an integral part of the forest. They are home to a host of cavity-dwelling wildlife. They break down over time and return important nutrients to the forest floor. If any particular defunct tree threatens the house, take it down. Otherwise, laissez-faire.

Once, back when a squirrel could run from Portland, Maine, to Beaumont, Texas, and never touch the ground, there were some defensible grounds for cutting forests. Most extra-urban dwellers back then were farmers, and if farmers wanted to plant corn, it was incumbent upon them to cut trees. Corn (like most grasses) doesn't abide shade.

There was also a safety factor to consider back in great-great-great-grandpappy's day. Say there really were two Native Americans in the glen and say their interest was not in forming a social compact with the new neighbor. A forest coming right up to the doorstep doesn't offer much visage or warning when company comes calling. It also detracts from the line of fire.

I sympathize with new homeowners who find the house of their dreams right in the middle of a newly leveled dirt plain. In similar circumstances, I'd probably ignore my better judgment and just slap a sod toupee down, too. (Who has time to wait a hundred years for a forest—or even ten years for a nice stand of saplings?)

But in the name of a naturally vegetated planet (and unencumbered weekends), I implore the designers of developments to leave the trees. Cut a circumspect access. And as unobtrusively as possible, just drop in the foundations.

Me? Well, I've recently initiated a little experiment. In the name of science, I decided to sacrifice a whopping section of lawn to see how long it will take for it to revert to a full-fledged meadow. With luck, and patience, I may even see a forest someday.

The Ultimate Joystick

"YOU WANT me to do what?" I asked, over the top of my drink, flashing a party grin.

"Hug a tree," Dale repeated, matching then eclipsing my best effort with a grin of her own—a wide, open, honest smile that has warmed many a preschooler's heart.

"Whatever for," I replied, studying my friend and New Jersey Audubon co-worker, trying to determine whether she was serious or not.

"Because it feels good," she said with a shrug and, if anything, a bigger smile than the one she'd donned before.

"I don't think so," I said, leaning back, against the trunk of an ancient butternut, feeling the rough bark pressing through my shirt. "It just feels rough and scratchy to me."

"You're thinking like a grown-up," Dale chided, "and you've forgotten a lot. Think about it," she encouraged, rising, leaving. "I'm going to go help Linda with the salad."

"Hug a tree," I thought, leaning back, taking another sip of my drink, shifting my position to one of greater comfort. "Hug a tree?"

We'd been talking about children and how substitute stimulation was supplanting real pleasure . . .

How video games were going to kill sandlot baseball and going fishing in the crick. How the nature programming was supplanting real hands-on experience with the natural world and setting up unrealistic expectations in the minds of those few people who do venture outside with the thought of experiencing nature firsthand.

"There's no defense against the stuff," I asserted. Video images prey on our senses. Stimulate nerves and release hormones just like real-life situations. Your clothes don't get dirty sliding into second, and the way TV viewers figure it, if the only thing you miss on the Nature Channel is the smell of an otter, well, it's no great loss.

"You missed something," Dale observed, not telling me what it was. Making me ask for it (an old teacher-naturalist's trick).

"What?" I asked (falling for it).

"Touch," she said, stretching like a tabby in the sun. "Feel." The ultimate interface with humans and the environment.

"Feel what?" I demanded. That's when Dale told me to go hug a tree.

The more I thought about it the more sense (so to speak) it made. We enter the world, an unbroken interfacing surface, and immediately start putting layers between us and the environment. It starts with swaddling clothes and ends with a shroud, and in between are snow suits that strangle and dress shoes that pinch and walls and malls and automobiles with tinted glass, power steering, and cruise control.

All our other senses—sight, sound, smell—are catered to. We buy tickets to exotic places to offer our eyes something new to feast upon. We tune in to the latest innovation in sound recording to excite our tympanic membrane. We sniff as we pass the bakery door or bury our noses in other people's roses.

But how the world *feels*, well, that only seems to matter when some discomfort threshold gets pushed—when we get cold and wet, when a summer heat wave banishes us to air-conditioned rooms, when the bark of the tree you are leaning up against starts making angry, red indentations in your back.

I shifted my position and shifted mental gears.

"Sure," I reasoned. A video game might be able to make a game out of shooting ducks. It can test eye-hand coordination and call up those old atavistic instincts. But can a video game offer a breeze blowing in your face, the cold touch of

frost on the sides of a duck blind, or the warm touch of sunlight on your cheeks that sends a shiver through your body?
No video game I've ever played.

If some company made a video game out of skipping
stones across a lake, could the feel of a perfect skipper be
replicated in a joystick? Can a mere game convey the cool,
smooth touch of stone or let you savor the potency of the
gravity-defying miracle enfolded in your hand?

Does a joystick make an arm stretch with pleasant
strain, let muscles grapple with gravity in the effort to break
earthly bonds? Can a mere game re-create that subtle fusion
between a finger and a stone that lets you know, as soon as
the skipper leaves your finger, that you've got a ten-splash
throw for sure?

We have even forgotten, it seems, the certain knowledge that lies in the mind of every fox and frog—that March
sunlight on a cold and windy day is one of the greatest tactile
treats in the universe. Try it and see.

Lie down in the lee of a hill, out of the wind, full in the
sun. Feel the prickle of last year's grass behind your ear; let
your fingers reach down to the new grass beneath. Now turn
your face to the sun and feel the strength of it. A March sun
is just as strong as a September sun (only the air overlying the
Northern Hemisphere is cooler).

Close your eyes and savor the molten glow of your
eyelids the way you did as a child. Turn your face to the
side, accepting both the grassy prickles on one cheek and
the warmth of the sun on the other. It's a regular sensory
overload.

"Hug a tree, huh," I mused.

I stood, turned, and regarded the butternut with its
quirky bark, all rough and smooth at the same time, wondering what the proper etiquette was, wondering what I would
say if anyone saw me. It has been a long time since I have
been so small and reached to hug a thing so big, but this long-
ing must lie very deep—even deeper than the instincts that
govern things like hunting ducks.

I placed my arms around the trunk, oddly pleased that
I could not make my fingers touch. Then, taking a quick

glance toward the house to make sure no one was watching, I closed both eyes and placed my cheek against the tree—and felt.

Felt the roughness that tickled and the smoothness that soothed. Felt the strength that was greater than my strength and the odd certainty that the tree did not mind the intrusion.

Felt that I had just encountered the ultimate joystick and that video game manufacturers have really got their work cut out for them if they are going to try to compete with something as simple and as grand as interfacing with nature, as hugging a tree.

TV Nature; Throwing Stones

THE SUBJECT is rocks. Rocks and television and what they have in common. Now you might think that these two elements have very little in common (and I can see how you may be right). The fact is, I know very little about rocks and less about television. In my next life, I aspire to be a geologist—or an astronaut, or a fighter pilot . . . In my next life, I'll strive to gain a working understanding of the television listings page in our local paper.

Oh, I know enough about rocks and television to get by. Igneous, metamorphic, sedimentary; ABC, NBC, CBS. If somebody hands me a piece of quartz and a piece of sandstone, I can distinguish them every time. If somebody asks me to turn on an unfamiliar television set, I can normally master the challenge in something under two minutes. But I can no more locate a designated cable television channel than I can launch a space probe (which, come to think of it, comes to the same thing).

So what do rocks and television have in common? Well, both tend to remain in a state of quiescence until some outside force works upon them. Both are foundations—one of mountains and streambeds, the other of modern culture. And both rocks and television may establish barriers to the natural world that are almost impossible to vault: rocks by piling up one atop another in the form of mountains, television by setting up a set of expectations that are impossible to meet.

How did I come upon my newfound understanding? By spending two weeks with a group of teenage birders, aged thirteen through seventeen, at a birding camp in Southeast Arizona. The fifteen teenagers were drawn from across the country. Neat kids.

Neat kids. Friendly, enthusiastic, earnest, and filled to the gunwales with curiosity and determination. They were at an age when a cresting blemish can shatter an ego and a dirty pair of socks on the floor or an open jar of peanut butter on the counter goes unseen. They could do things with a Frisbee that physics is still trying to bind by theory, and they could bird with skills that even many accomplished adults might envy.

They also threw stones. Lots of them. Every chance they got.

Stone throwing is an ancient art and an essential part of easing into adulthood. I don't pretend to understand all the forces that trigger the stone-throwing response in pubescent males. A friend, a ranger in the Tetons named Katy, whose job it is to keep kids from chucking rocks at the ground squirrels, calls it "testosterone poisoning."

I just know that whenever a group of teenage boys stands around long enough in one place, outdoors, a period of communal stone chucking usually ensues. "Stand around long enough in one place" is another way of saying "get bored."

It's possible that the proximity of one or two teenage girls acts as a catalyst to stone chucking, but this needs to be tested. And before some feminist hard-liner accuses me of all kinds of unkind things, let me hasten to add that the best stone chucker I ever knew was my old neighborhood chum, Donna. Donna could peg any runner trying to reach home plate from any point in the outfield, and she was never known to get any less than ten skips from a stone skimmed across a lake. It's possible that girls just pass through the stone-chucking stage earlier than boys. Donna's career crested when she was ten.

Back to boys.

This was the usual pattern of our daily outings. We'd arrive at a designated birding location and search for target birds (figuratively speaking). We'd hunt as a pack, adults and subadults, senses alert, movements guided by purpose. And then the great shout would go up.

"There it is. Keyed up. In the pale green bush next to the big rock. High on the left side."

There would be pandemonium—scramble and panic and cries of "where?" "where?" and occasionally "ow" as some cat-clawed branch raked a bare leg. Eventually the panicked pleas for direction would be replaced by gratified shouts of "WOW" and "BRUTAL" and "AWESOME."

Then, after a period of intense admiration (lasting about as long as your average television commercial), the group would, well, sort of lose its cohesiveness. The kids would wander off. A spirited period of stone chucking would ensue. And then everyone would pile into the vans and wait for the adults to get their act together and take them someplace else.

Incidentally, don't get the idea that this was malicious stone chucking. This was benign stone chucking. Not a rock was thrown in anger. Not a stop sign or garbage can or (heaven forbid) a bird was designated the target. Most of the stones were directed toward lakes and streams, which produced satisfying "plops" and ripples for each well-thrown chucking stone and serial "splishes" for artfully thrown skippers.

What I gleaned from watching this group of young birders was this: for most, their attention span was shorter rather than longer. Long-term study and appreciation of things, even things that they were intensely interested in, did not seem to be their forte. The other thing I surmised was that inactivity was anathema to them. Sitting or standing in one place for too long seemed to grate on their souls.

But all this changed when we got back to the motel to sit out the heat of the day. The television sets went on, and teenage energy levels plummeted. *Gilligan's Island* and *I Dream of Jeannie* reruns did what no blue grosbeak or painted redstart could. They mesmerized the troops. They turned the whole lot of them into sedentary little stones.

Now, I can pretty much visualize your agreeing with me that television is ruining young lives (but not your life). How you support public television and only turn on the tube to

watch the National Geographic Specials and all the neat nature programs. Well, that's dandy. Now, let me introduce you
to the dark side of the force.

The problem with nature programs is that they set up
expectations that cannot possibly be met in nature. Television
gives viewers an intimacy with bats and birds and army ants
that is greater than life—which is another way of saying, it
isn't real.

Television takes you right into the marsupial's pouch in
Australia; it captures every detail of the lion's kill in Kenya
and the bald eagle's flight in Alaska. It shows things, in thirty-
minute segments, that require hundreds and thousands of
hours and patience in real time, in real *life*, to observe.

Why is this bad? Because now, when people leave the
sheltered confines of their home entertainment centers and
venture into the real world in search of nature, they expect
to find nature as they saw it on the screen. When they go to
a national park or a local reservoir to see wintering eagles,
they expect to see a mob of eagles—eating salmon, courting,
building nests, raising young, learning to fly, all at point-
blank range. The single, somnambulant eagle perched three
hundred yards away just doesn't meet their expectations. It
just does not pack the punch of television nature programs.

There is another problem. When people see nature in
all its edited and enhanced glory on television and don't find
it at command at their backdoor, they get the mistaken impression that nature is something that exists far, far away.
In places like Australia, Kenya, and Alaska. They forget, if
they ever realized, that nature takes time and that eagles in
Massachusetts and in Missouri do everything that eagles in
Alaska do. Only television eagles do everything in thirty minutes or less.

When this happens, the value of natural areas lying
close at hand becomes diminished in people's minds. They
become not as rich as other places. They become *not worth
saving*, and this sadly becomes a self-fulfilling prophecy because habitat not worth saving has a way of becoming *gone*.

When this happens, there is nothing left to do but sit
indoors and watch reruns of *Gilligan's Island*. Or perhaps just
throw stones.

Zen and the Art of Throwing Metal

GRASS CLUTCHED at the bottom of the gate, but I was adamant, and the weathered latticework finally opened wide enough to let me slip by. I didn't trouble to close it. I didn't think it would stand the strain.

There used to be a path here, and my feet tried to find it. But the weeds that choked the lane and the unpruned tree limbs throwing combination punches at my head proved that pedestrian traffic had fallen off of late. "At least," I thought, "I won't have to ask anyone's leave to fish through."

The dock (if three planks leading out over a pond make a dock) was in the same state of disrepair as the gate. It shuddered when I tested it with a foot and shook as if the pilings were grounded in gelatin when I trusted it with my weight. Ripples spread and collided across the surface of the pond. Small sunfish drew near to see what all the commotion was about, and half a dozen frogs held their collective breaths and made small wagers.

But the pilings held, and I held to my ambition, and there I was, at the end of the dock, with a fishing rod in one hand and a tackle box in the other. Before me (and beneath me) was a half-acre farm pond . . . and whatever fortune it might contain.

It hardly seems necessary to explain, at this point, that I planned to wet a line, but it's not as simple or as straightforward as you think. Fact is, I don't fish—not anymore. Yes, once, long ago, I was an enthusiastic fisherman, and most of my allowance money still lies embedded right to the shank in the submerged stumps that lie beneath the Brick Yard Ponds to prove it. But soon after college, the murder of bass and the thrill of one-sided tugs of war with trough-reared trout ceased to captivate me. Maybe the growing complexities of life just crowded fishing out, but I think what happened was that I simply reached a point where I didn't need to define myself by seeking dominion over cold-blooded things. Mind you I've got nothing against fishing. It's just that fishing doesn't do much for me anymore. When I have a hankering for a nice filet, well, I save my money and buy one. When I need an excuse to enjoy a day afield or chum up with the guys, I usually go birding.

So, what was I doing at the end of a rickety dock with a fishing rod in my hand? Posing for the cover of *Gray's Sporting Journal*? No. Actually, I was there to throw metal. To many, the art of throwing metal, of spin fishing with lures, is the art of fishing, but this is not inevitably so, and this is what I hope to explain. Throwing metal is a skill, an art. It is Zen.

Throwing metal is, at once, a discipline of body and mind and a cosmic reach of the soul. It combines the grace of a ballerina and the eye of an archer. It brings out the Sparky Lyle in a person and the Mother Teresa too.

Throwing metal has little to do with that crude utilitarian practice known as "bait fishing." And though it shares kinship with fly fishing, it differs in one key respect. When casting a fly, there is time to second guess, to adjust, to redirect the direction of a cast. With fly fishing, you sort of ease the lure into perfection.

But throwing metal is a single, precise leap of faith— total perfection or total failure, all or nothing. All . . .

Alone. At the end of the dock, you direct your ambition down the narrow length of graphite and will the sliver of metal along the course laid down by your will. Your eyes fasten upon some point in the featureless pool. You raise your rod like a swordsman saluting a worthy opponent. The graphite blade flexes, taunting gravity . . . and then . . . at the one precise moment when gravity knows defeat, you bring your wrist forward. The rod springs to life. Your finger releases the gossamer-fine line. The silver sliver arches like a catcher's throw to second. The line sings through the air.

And with a plop that hardly troubles the tranquillity of the pond, the lure disappears beneath the surface.

The best part of all is the retrieve. After a well-directed cast, you get to reel in the lure—a nice, slow, even retrieve. It's a lot better than just chucking rocks into a pond because you don't have to keep finding more rocks.

While the silver sliver dances and shines beneath the surface, it releases your mind to wander in thought or to savor the pleasure of nothing at all. There is bliss in the retrieve. There is freedom. Even Sisyphus, standing atop his mountain and unfettered by his boulder, knows no greater freedom than this.

This, of course, is the Socratic idea. In throwing metal as in most other worldly pursuits, the reality often falls short. Or long. There is a bad tendency to overshoot when throwing metal. If your imaginary target is, say, out beyond some ocean jetty or out in the middle of a thousand-acre reservoir, no problem. But let there be a single overhanging limb or the most insignificant submerged stump anywhere within the limits of a full spool, and sooner or later even the most artfully directed lure is going to find it.

What chance does Zen have in the face of accident and chance?

Not only does snagging some stump steal the pleasure of a retrieve; it's likely to cost you a lure and lots of fishing line (which is amazingly expensive stuff for something you can't even see). If your hook is firmly embedded and your monofilament line made to handle those lunkers, your Zen-like tranquillity may be sorely tested. This means you can get so mad that you end up splintering the tip of your rod.

A greater risk to "just throwing metal" lurks beneath the surface of the pond. No matter how good your intentions, no matter how lackluster your retrieve, there is always some fish, somewhere, who is dumb enough to try to grab a lure and ruin the tranquillity.

The art of losing fish, once they are hooked, is an obscure branch of lore little practiced today. I have read many books directed toward catching fish but none that deal with losing them. Much of what I know of this subject I have had to learn by myself.

It pays, first of all, to make sure your hooks are dull. Sharp hooks embed quickly—before you or the fish can react. Dull hooks give the fish a chance to spit out the tasteless piece of metal before it's too late.

You can also file the barbs off the hooks. This makes it easier for a fish, once inadvertently hooked, to work itself free. Patience is all that is required from your end. Patience and a slack line.

But perhaps the greatest obstacle to those seeking attainment in the art of throwing metal is the conservation officer. Explaining to conservation officers the subtle differences between mere fishing (which requires a license) and the art of throwing metal, which is a religion and therefore tax exempt, is no small art in itself.

Invariably, right in the middle of your explanation about the separation of church and state, some stupid, agnostic bass is going to grab the sliver of metal and behave like a fish fighting for its life.

Only a true Zen master can maintain tranquillity in the face of such incontrovertible evidence. Neophytes, seeking attainment through the art of throwing metal, would be advised to buy a fishing license—just in case.

Revenge of the Jabberwock

AT LAST it was finished. He examined the polished wand with a critical eye, savoring the weight of it and feeling its potency.

"Now if that's not a vorpal sword, I've never seen one," he thought proudly.

It's not likely that anyone was going to argue the point. First, there was no one else around. Second, Lewis Carroll is probably the only person with standing to contradict the assertion, and he's not telling. (For all anyone knows, one lean, mean scraped and polished switch from a sumac bush in the hands of an eight-year-old might be precisely what a vorpal sword is.) And, finally, only a fool is going to contradict a kid whipped into a romantic frenzy who's holding a stick in his hand.

Leaving the shredded mound of bark and sawdust on the workbench ("I'll clean it up later," he promised), he stepped into the backyard for an initial test firing. No space center engineer ever held greater expectations.

"*Snicker-snack!*" he yelled.

"*Whoosh,*" went the stick.

"Hmmmm, doesn't sound quite right." He tried it again. "*Snicker-snack!!!*"

"*Whoosh,*" the stick insisted.

He tried choking up a bit on his grip, but this didn't generate the aspired-to special effects either.

"Maybe it's all in the wrist," he speculated. To test this,

he tried putting a full-throttled sweep into quick reverse and learned painfully a lesson relating to bodies in motion—and how they tend to stay in motion—another way of saying that when you swing a stick one way and try to make it go the other way, it hurts your wrist.

He decided to try a little more forward thrust. Grasping the imaginary blade with both hands, he gave the stick a full-bodied swing that described a 360-degree arc.

"Snicker-snack!" he yelled.

"Whoosh . . . snap!" went the vorpal blade.

He studied the decapitated rose bush with a mixture of pride and horror.

"Well, at least I know it works," he rationalized. "You wouldn't want to go and do battle with a Jabberwock with an untested blade." Surely his mother would understand *that* (he hoped).

It's a wise commander who knows when it's time to quit the field. Clearly this was one of those times.

"Long time the manxome foe he sought." En route, he had several clashes with some rather treacherous-looking stands of goldenrod, and there was one furious engagement with a pokeberry bush that was at least twice his size.

So deep was his battle frenzy that it was only later, after the bush was completely trashed, that he realized he had been wounded in the battle. On his shirt, the one he should have taken off when he got home from school, was a blood-red berry stain.

"It's almost impossible to defend yourself against a suicide attack," he reasoned. "Maybe it will come out in the wash."

Several times he caught sight of what were almost certainly Jubjub birds. At one point, he felt pretty sure that a fruminous Bandersnatch was stalking him. But the Bandersnatch hasn't been born that will risk being Keilbabed by a vorpal blade.

Actually, he rather wished that some Bandersnatch would make a try for him. It was pretty clear that he had missed the afternoon lineup of Jabberwocks, and, frankly, he was getting bored.

The battle with the pokeberry had been fun. He wished he'd find another. Goldenrod really wasn't much sport. The stems were too stringy. No matter how much imagination you lavished on it, a stick was still a stick, and sticks don't cut goldenrod very easily. You sort of have to beat them to the ground, and there's no artistry in that.

In a marshy area beside the bank of what used to be an elevated railroad bed, he came upon a thriving stand of spotted touch-me-nots. The vaselike flowers were turning red with the lateness of the season, and the fat, full-bodied seed pods were so ripe that they burst of their own accord. The slightest touch sent patterns of seeds firing in all directions.

"Now there's a formidable adversary," he thought happily. "A plant that shoots back."

The flanks of the well-armed succulent were protected by greenbrier. A dangerous frontal attack seemed his only option.

"*One, two! One, two! And through and through. The vorpal blade went snicker-snack!*"

Flowers flew. Seed pods detonated. Honeybees fled the scene. Row after row of plants fell to his assault. A smell, like uncooked vegetables, filled the air, fueling his wrath.

He hated vegetables.

He waded in among the fallen plants, heedless of the vegetable gore that was making a royal mess of his new $150 sneakers.

From the corner of one eye, he saw one plant standing. He spun, catching it smartly at the base.

Dangerous to leave your rear unguarded.

More and more, he cut. His arm began to ache with the effort. Small vines that grew amid the stalks dragged at his blade. Dead tree branches hidden among the lush growth sent jarring shock waves rolling up the stick, into his hand.

"Ow!"

Finally, it was over. With a mighty slash, the last and most formidable of the plants (probably their captain) surrendered to his blade. He stood, panting, surveying the enemies that had fallen to his skill with a blade. No conquering captain with whole armies at his command ever surveyed a victory with more pride.

The groundhog was halfway across the mutilated clearing before it saw the boy and the boy saw it. Both were startled.

The groundhog was a youngster. This was its first fall. In a few short weeks, it would be going into hibernation in the den whose entrance was set in the old railroad bed—just behind the strange intruder. This presented a dilemma.

The intruder was large and potentially dangerous, something to be avoided. But safety, the entrance to its den, necessitated walking past this creature. It certainly was a dilemma.

The boy had a different problem. It had never really occurred to him that he might actually *find* a Jabberwock. Plants are one thing. But . . .

That is, he'd never . . .

And what if . . . ?

The groundhog made up its mind first. Dropping to all fours, the football-sized rodent made straight for the den, straight for the boy. As strategies go, this one is more likely to get you written into a poem than win you a battle, but very few groundhogs are accounted among the world's great military strategists.

Even though the boy knew that this was precisely the attack plan favored by Jabberwocks, the suddenness of it took him by surprise. He jumped to one side—that is, he feigned to the left (which given the circumstances was not a bad thing to do). And as the rogue Jabberwock *"came whiffling through the tulgey wood"* and drew abreast, the boy's gratitude at realizing that the beast was not really attacking manifested itself in a decision to let bygones be bygones—a withdrawal with honor.

Except, at the last moment, it occurred to him that this might be the only Jabberwock he would ever get a crack at. That cowardice was something he couldn't live with. That right and might were clearly on his side. *And* that the Jabberwock had made a serious tactical blunder. It had turned its back on him.

The vorpal blade went snicker-snack. And again. And again. And again . . .

Perhaps groundhogs are made of sterner stuff than Jabberwocks, or perhaps killing things is not as simple, nor as easy, as poets and politicians make it out to be. Most boys discover this hard and ugly truth when they are very young; some, when they are a bit older.

But then, at some point, when young boys become old, old men, they seem to forget again. I often wonder why.

He left the Jabberwock dead, but unlike the poem, he declined to make a trophy of its head. And if "galumphing" means he walked very slowly and felt sick to his stomach, well, then, he went galumphing back.

That night, in bed, he contemplated what a month without television and with extra weekend chores was going to be like—punishment for a list of atrocities that merely began with the mess left in the workshop. He didn't mention it to anyone, but the punishments actually made him feel better.

The next morning, a hummingbird came to the violated stand of flowers to feed. It tried some of the trampled plants, but the blossoms were dead and drained of nectar. It left, still hungry.

Dialogue with Ms. D'Vil

THE SEATED FIGURE in the hooded windbreaker turned, revealing a woman's face, and morning sunlight fell upon features that were delicate and fine—except for her mouth. The mouth was generous, smiling and inviting. She was pretty—yes, *pretty* is the word that described her. If you'd passed on the street, if you'd studied her from across the room at some party, that is how you might recall her.

Unless you looked in her eyes. The eyes were cold and lifeless, two holes cut into a dark universe beyond reason and sanity. All the warmth of a spring sunrise fell upon those eyes and died there, and I shivered as, deep in my mind, Irish ghosts set up a keening.

"Mr. Dunne," she said, nodding, smiling widely to reveal porcelain-fine teeth that looked as if they'd been filed.

I'm used to people that I can't place knowing who I am. I do a lot of public speaking, and my memory stinks. But I knew, beyond question or doubt, that even in a crowd of five hundred people I wouldn't have overlooked or forgotten *this* face and *these* eyes.

"I'm sorry," I began, "but I don't believe I know you or . . ."

"Don't you?" she admonished. "My name is D'Vil, Jersey D'Vil. But you can call me Jerry. Lovely view," she invited, changing the subject, turning her eyes upon the Sussex County landscape below us.

I followed her gaze, taking in the forest and farmland

parcels along with the disturbing numbers of houses, shopping centers, professional buildings, and highways that were rapidly transforming this once pristine corner of New Jersey into a suburban patchwork.

"Yes," I agreed. "It is lovely—still. But ten years ago, the view from this spot was like a calendar snapshot—nothing but forest and farmland."

She giggled, a quick, down-scale giggle that never left her throat.

"It's the development," I explained. "People can't afford to buy closer to the city, and the region's natural heritage is being swept away. The land is being chopped into bits and pieces. It's happening without rhyme or reason, and it's happening too fast for people and communities and governments to come to grips with it. It's a crisis—the biggest crisis this state has ever faced."

She chortled! A low, choppy laugh that sounded like axes falling in the forest.

"If something isn't done quickly, any reason to live in this state is going to be destroyed."

And the creature threw back her head and howled like Cerberus. She laughed and laughed until her eyes were wet with tears that refused to fall. "Ah, me," she said, recovering, "ah, me. Wait till you see it in ten years. It's going to make Silicon Valley look like it should fall under the jurisdiction of the National Park Service."

I stared. Stunned. I started to utter a denial, but the words died in my throat. "Who are you?" I stammered.

She only smiled, then stood, and it was then that I noticed her feet. She was tall, but her shoes would have fit a child.

"A family trait," she explained without being asked. "All the Leeds have small feet."

I started at the sound of the name, a name of ill omen in the annals of Pine Barrens legend and lore.

"You come from South Jersey?" I inquired.

"Originally," she said, stretching like a cat. "But I travel a lot these days—work all over the country in fact."

"And just what do you do?" I probed.

She didn't say anything for a while. She merely studied me with those eyes that took all the sunlight out of the world. "Haven't you guessed?" she said in low, even tones. "I'm a . . . ah . . . *planner*. A planner," she repeated, delighted for some reason of her own. "*The* planner if you like. The post was open, and nobody else seemed interested so I took it on."

And she laughed, again—high-ringing laughter that sounded like the phone that rings deep in the night heralding sorrow and loss.

"Would you be interested in hearing an overview of my master plan?" she offered. And without waiting for an answer, the master planner gave me her vision for the future. It was a future as sterile as an empty picture tube and as hopeful as a fall from the gallows.

There were faceless corporate buildings that were vessels of routine and unbroken plains crowded with houses and streets that never knew the sound of feet in play. What, after all, was the sense of going outside? There was nothing to do there.

There were malls whose interiors were designed to mimic natural areas with ponds and trees, and if you could stomach the hours in traffic, there were airports that offered the too brief comfort of travel to some unspoiled corner of the planet. Yes, there were parks. Overly manicured parcels stripped clean of living things, whose rules and procedures cut the heart out of anything that might challenge a child's mind or soothe a troubled adult soul. There were natural areas too—a few. They were jealously guarded, accessible by permit and privilege.

As I listened and watched and saw her vision unfold, I hated her—*hated* her for forcing me to face this future in my lifetime. But my hatred was, I knew, only a shadow compared to the hatred our descendants would direct at us should we allow such a future to happen.

The words and vision had stopped. I turned and studied her, studying me.

"Why are you telling me this?"

She only raised her arms over her head, stretched, smiled, and made a happy sound deep in her throat.

"We won't let it happen," I said. "The American people consistently vote for green issue candidates. The American people demand a strong environmental policy."

She smiled.

"Open space is part of our heritage. It helped mold our national character. It is important to the recreational needs of everyone who lives in this country."

She smiled.

"There are a lot of people who have a major stake in the future of America, including some of the richest corporations in the world. They're not going to gamble their resources away on a country that is going to let itself go all to hell. They know what a sterile environment will do to worker productivity. We won't let it happen."

"You will," she purred.

"What makes you so sure?" I demanded.

And she laughed again. She laughed so loud and long that all living things within earshot begged for the mercy of silence.

"You will," she said. "Because you always have. Because the kids need shoes . . . because the lawn needs cutting . . . because the car is running funny . . . because the mortgage is due . . . and the stockholders want a profit . . . and the economy is sluggish and can't accommodate any more environmental controls, right now.

"You will," she said, again, "because the everyday problems of everyday living are pressing and manifest, while problems with the environment are abstract, contestable, and easily deferred."

"What would you do if you were me?" I asked, playing devil's advocate.

"What would I do?" she mimicked, feigning concentration. "Let's see. I'd write to my federal and state representatives, demanding that more money be allocated for land preservation. And I'd clog every tabloid in this country with letters to the editor demanding large natural areas be set aside to preserve natural heritage.

"And I'd demand that environmental education become part of every school curriculum, that people be taught that the environment is not one interest conflicting with others. It is the foundation upon which all decisions and human endeavors must rest."

"Why are you telling me this? You know I'll write an essay warning people what the future holds."

"Oh, Mr. Dunne," she mocked, "of course you will. Why do you think I set up this meeting? Of course, you'll tell them."

Then her face twisted into a mask that made even the death in her eyes seem like mercy, and her voice pitched until it cut like a chainsaw. "And then they won't even be able to stand before their children and plead that they didn't know it was happening. You'll tell them. And they'll know. And when they do nothing, they will deserve the future they get.

"Well," she said abruptly. "Sorry to cut this short, but there's a senatorial hearing involving the Endangered Species Act I need to attend."

With a wink and a wave, she turned and started down the trail leaving tiny footprints in her wake. But just before hitting the main road, she turned and shouted, "Oh, listen, for your article, it's D'Vil with a capital *V*. O.K.?"

I nodded.

She shouted something else that was taken and scattered by the wind. I'm not certain, but if I had to guess, if someone wanted to know, I think it might have been "Have a nice day."

Cruelty and Turtles

WE TURNED the corner and saw it there, a soft-ball-sized lump of hard-shelled determination—a turtle on the wrong side of the road. The Cumberland County, New Jersey, lane that friend Don and I were traveling doesn't see ten cars an hour but . . .

"We've got to stop, Peter," Don announced—I might add, unnecessarily. My foot was already reaching for the brake.

"I'll get it," Don said, and he did. Jumped from the car before it came to a stop. Ran toward the uncomprehending terrapin. Snatched it from harm's way.

Then, turtle in hand, he crossed the road, deposited it on the opposing side, and got back in the car.

"Pretty one," was all he said, all that needed to be said.

"Yes," I agreed. "It was a pretty one."

This essay is about box turtles. Turtles and kindness and its dark twins, cruelty and malice, but mostly it's about turtles. And what I know about them. And what they mean to me. And why.

The truth is that I know very little about box turtles if you equate knowledge with biological facts, but I am content with this. I know that, like most reptiles, box turtles hatch from eggs. I know that they like to eat wild strawberries. I know that if you catch a box turtle and put it in a shoe box on your dresser, it will scratch at the box all night trying to escape until, sick with guilt and sleeplessness, you will release it in the morning.

If you don't release it, your mother almost certainly will. With the possible exception of sons and daughters and florists, box turtles have more reason to celebrate Mother's Day than any other creatures alive.

What I know and love most of all about the creature is that box turtles have magic hinges on the bottom of their shells that let them shut out the world. It's what biologists call a defense mechanism.

This defense mechanism helps little box turtles grow up and become big box turtles. It gives box turtles a place to hide when a hungry raccoon or fox approaches. It keeps box turtles safe from harm if they reach for a strawberry that is just out of reach and end up tumbling down a streambank.

The armored box works so well, in fact, that box turtles have grown somewhat oblivious to cruelty and danger, and isn't this ironic? That a creature's greatest strength should become its greatest weakness, its greatest liability. This is why the invention of the automobile and the lawn mower came as such a surprise to turtles. This is why human cruelty combined with human ingenuity blindsides box turtles every time.

Box turtles, you see, don't run when a car approaches. They don't fight. Why, they don't even look left and right before crossing the road.

When a car approaches, box turtles just hide, right there, on the highway, confident right down to the last hereditary gene that they are safe from harm inside their box.

And sometimes they are. If someone like Don is behind the wheel. If I am behind the wheel.

But sometimes, too many times, they are not safe. Sometimes they are killed by a misguided tire and inattentiveness on the part of the driver. This is sad. And sometimes they are killed by tires guided by cruelty and malice. This is appalling.

I know less about cruelty and malice than I know about box turtles, but I know that these dark qualities exist because, like turtles, like most people, I have been blindsided, too.

But even before being cruelty's victim, I was its witness. Back when I was young. Back in the turtle-catching years. It happened this way.

I was with a group of kids I called friends because my vocabulary was more limited then and because at the time I thought everyone you knew was a friend. Someone found a box turtle. And everyone passed it around and admired it. And then, of course, everyone wanted it "for keeps," but, of course, not everyone could have it.

There was too much ambition and not enough turtle to satisfy it, you see. There was too much jealousy and too much greed and not enough wisdom and very little restraint. So little by little—by taunt, by dare, by double-dare—it was decided that no one would have the turtle.

And then I learned about cruelty.

Later, at home, I went down into the basement and searched for and found the darkest and most secret corner. And I pulled my knees up to my chest. And I rested my chin upon my hands. And I stared at the darkness. And wished, with all my heart, that I had a shell with a trapdoor that I could close upon the world.

Later, years later, in fact, I learned that cruelty is not shed with childhood. That as people grow older, cruelty sometimes evolves into something more appalling still. This is malice.

There was another box turtle. This one was in the south-bound lane of a two-lane highway, and it was in its defensive position. There were no cars to be discomfited by my swerve to the shoulder, so I drew to a stop and ran back along the highway to rescue the hapless terrapin. The run became a race.

I don't know how I knew that the approaching car intended to run over the turtle—but I did know. Maybe I heard the engine rev or saw the car accelerate. Maybe the trajectory of the vehicle shifted, or perhaps I saw the face of the driver and read the intentions there.

The race ended in a tie, which, according to the rules governing such engagements, meant the driver won. He had the great sad pleasure he sought. He succeeded in mulching the turtle in front of my eyes, in front of my outstretched hand. He drove on, warmed by whatever it is that cruelty and malice release in people who worship or are enslaved by them.

As I said before, I find it difficult to understand cruelty and malice, cannot understand what it is about being the instrument of death and pain that is gratifying and alluring. And it is not for lack of contemplation. This is a subject I ponder a great deal.

Even more puzzling, I wonder why it is that our species seems divided between those who would go out of their way to run down an animal trapped on the highway and those like Don and me who go out of their way to prevent it.

And while you are puzzling over this dichotomy, let me toss another ingredient into the contemplative stew. Both Don and I are hunters, intimate with the ancient pageant that binds two living things and unbinds the poles of existence. Even so, even with the insight afforded a predator, I cannot understand how pleasure can be drawn from killing nor have I ever felt it.

Those people who run down turtles with cars, who wield death carelessly, callously, and for reasons that go beyond the reach of my understanding, well, I don't know what they are. Or why. My own understanding and respect for death makes me blind to their motives. Like the turtle within its shell, I don't understand.

Perhaps this is as it should be. Perhaps I should be grateful. Because it is possible that the only way to understand cruelty is to be cruel. And if this is so, then I plead for ignorance.

And I will stop, when and wherever I can, to help a turtle across the road. To honor its right to remain ignorant; to do what I can to balance the cruelty that exists in the world, though I do not understand it.

For a Tide

BETWEEN the Jersey pines and Delaware Bay is a great wetlands in league with, but less celebrated than the great salt marshes of the Chesapeake. In summer, these estuaries are lush and green; in autumn, lush and gold. They rise and fall with the tide, and the people who live there have taken this rhythm and woven it into the fabric of their lives.

In a town astride a river, in a house mantled by towering oaks, is the Camp family. Every September and October, for four generations, the Camps have hired out to itinerant gunners. When the tide is full and the birds are in, they pole their clients through flooded marshes "for a tide."

Teddy Roosevelt, I am told, hunted the marshes of Delaware Bay; maybe he was pushed by a Camp. Thomas Eakins, the famous Philadelphia painter, was in love with the pageantry of "poling" or "pushing," and he depicted this style of hunting no less than six times.

What kind of quarry can inspire the adoration of presidents and painters and place them in collusion with New Jersey baymen? Why, the sora (rail)—a shy, secretive marsh bird that launches itself with the lethargy of a Saturn Rocket, flies like the Wright Brothers, and soars in the esteem of those with epicurean palates.

"Rail birds" are small, hardly larger than a snipe. But the bag limit (the number of rails a gunner might legally take) is generous. Twenty-five birds!—an incredible number in this age, when a single black duck or canvasback constitutes the legal limit.

It's a number that almost recalls the limitless, free-for-all hunting that flourished in the last century—before ignorance and tasteless Victorian excess reduced whole populations of birds to remnants (and memories). But rail birds were spared the worst effects of unregulated hunting. Gunning's "Golden Age" passed them by, leaving their numbers intact.

Why? Well, as I said, the birds are secretive, and flight seems something of an afterthought to a rail. They are also solitary creatures. Sandpipers, close cousins to rails, fly in tight-packed flocks, lending themselves to slaughter. But one shot, no matter how strategic, cannot decimate legions of rails. In fact, and often enough, it cannot find one.

It is only when the river waters swell with the tide so that the flat-bottomed boats can navigate stands of wild rice that the birds can be hunted at all. And in the towns that cling to the marshes of Delaware Bay, there are baymen who may still be found, who understand the lore of rail hunting, and who may be hired to push you.

For a tide.

If you ask Ken Camp what time you should get down to the river, he'll look at the tide chart and ponder and say 8:00 (or 10:00 or 2:00, depending, of course, upon the date). If you call a month later to reconfirm, the time may change by fifteen minutes or so. Unlike airplane flight departures and prearranged conference calls, there is latitude in a tide.

So you get to the river at 2:00 (or 2:15) and meet the others who have come. Together you stand and make the small talk of men who do not know each other and watch the river and the stick that one of you shoved into the bank—watching the water climb the stick, willing it to rise higher.

Then the pickup trucks rattle down the mud rut road, and there are more introductions and then more waiting. Finally the boats are laid in the water. The baymen heft the long, use-slickened poles that they will use to propel the boats, getting the feel of them.

The gunners are assigned—one to a boat. They take their place in the bow, laying their guns beside them. In the stern, the boatmen lay into their paddles and begin the trip upriver where the beds and birds are found.

As the river takes you, as you slip your moorings to this century and fall back into the last, your boatman explains the things you will need to know.

"We'll line up and go through the beds together."

"O.K."

"The birds will most likely flush when we reach the end."

"All right."

"If I call 'mark,' it's a rail bird."

"Yes."

"'Hold,' you don't shoot."

And maybe, as you travel up the river with the tide, you will learn something of this other man's life. Where he lives. What he does for wages. Whether he is married and how many children he has. He, in turn, learns something of you and your life—whatever truths or half-truths you care to spend.

In the process, you take each other's measure. You, after all, will need his wisdom and skill. He will rely on your eye and your judgment. If your qualities match, by the time you reach the stands of rice, you are a team.

The boats pause at the outer stalks, frozen like birds poised for flight. Poles replace the paddles in the boatmen's hands. Gunners stand, and a voice commands, "Load up."

The polers steady their boats, and for a time the air rings with the sound of metal on metal. The singing ring of shell sliding into the chamber of an autoload. The sharp, no-nonsense "clack-clack" of a pump gun engulfing a shell. The latch soft "snap" of a double being closed. Then the polers lean into their poles, and the slender boats edge through the rice.

If the tides are full-moon high or boosted by a storm swell, the poler's job is easy, and the boats glide like scud. But when the tide is near the low point of its cycle or if the winds are wrong and strong, the going is difficult, and polers must work hard for small gains.

The rice closes in around you. The other gunners in their flanking boats are reduced to disembodied heads and shoulders. But your eyes are fixed on the grass and the water that lie ahead. Even the migrating hawks passing close, or a speeding flock of teal, or the distant sound of guns reaching out across the marsh does not distract you.

Suddenly the reeds move, and dark wings flutter. A voice behind shouts "Mark!" then "HOLD! Hold!" And you watch the blackbird arch overhead, to land somewhere behind. Only then do you remember to breathe.

The boats glide like stalking cats, one push pole length at a time. They pause before the last of the rice and the open water that lies a push pole length away.

"Be ready when we reach the edge," your bayman says, and you nod.

Then one of the boats noses forward, and you feel your boatman put his weight to his pole. The message is carried through the boat. You can feel it through your feet. You can feel it in the blood.

There is a momentary lag between the time a boatman leans on his pole and the point at which a boat moves forward. It is just enough time to cast a look around. To marvel at how blue a sky can be. To note how sharp the wind sounds when it moves through the grass. To appreciate how singular a privilege it is to live, now, at the end of this century and know kinship with presidents and painters and baymen who lived in the last.

And to be able to find a boatman. On the great estuaries of Delaware Bay. Who knows the lore of rails and who will push you across flooded marshes.

For a tide.

Then the boat edges forward, and you must clear your mind of all other things. Because it is time. And there is no time.

Falling in Ernest

IT WAS WARM, but nobody could have mistaken it for anything but a morning in November. Two days of rain had washed autumn out of the hillsides, though here and there you could still find patches of color—the burnished crown of a hardy oak, the crimson banner brandished by a particularly resilient maple.

But for the most part, what little color the hills could claim they could thank the yellows for—the sweet gums, the willows, and the tulip poplars. When the rain stopped, it was clear that the reds had quit the field. But the yellows still hung in there, tough and proud.

Leaves don't lead especially exciting or glamorous lives. For six months or so, mid-May through September, things are patently routine, life at the sugar mines, seven days a week, dawn till dusk, converting sunlight into food energy. The work's not all that tough. Heck, any leaf can do it. But it *is* monotonous, and there isn't a whole lot to chat about, since everyone on the branch is doing pretty much the same thing. In fact, in the life of your average leaf, there is just one break with routine. That is the day it falls; six months of service and sacrifice for a big fifteen seconds of free-fall. Sisyphus with a short-term contract.

It's not a lot to show for all that work, but if one drop is all you get, you'd best make the most of it. At least, that's the way this particular leaf figured it.

He was a tulip leaf and a damn fine one—bigger and

burlier than most, broad at the blade, narrow at the stem. A simple leaf (nothing compound about him).

Good fortune had given him a spot near the top of a particularly fine tulip poplar, one of the tallest northeastern hardwoods. He had a great view of the ridge, the farm, the pond below. He had a good attitude. And he had just one ambition: to make his jump a good one. So the leaf spent all of his spare time studying techniques. He'd been studying since the first leaf began to fall in September.

The birches and poplars went first. Why, frost wasn't even a rumor when the whole pack turned color and shivered their way to the ground.

"No guts," the tulip leaf concluded.

The hickories and maples were next. Oh, they talked a good war, but when the first frost hit back in 25 (i.e., October 25) they couldn't hit the ground fast enough.

"A real mob scene, a rout," the leaf recalled bitterly. "The whole lot just bailed out. It was pretty embarrassing. But we were all pretty green back then," he admitted quietly to himself.

The oaks hung in there for a while. "Oaks are a fine tree," the tulip leaf thought. "If I had to be another leaf, I'd be an oak. But I'm glad I'm a tulip. A tulip's a damn fine tree."

Mostly it was the tulips holding their colors now. "And the willow across the pond," the tulip leaf noted without much friendliness. The tulip leaf couldn't feel very good about a tree that spent all of its time looking down at its own reflection. "And that group of hemlocks on the opposite hill-side," he added.

He didn't know the hemlocks, and he didn't much like them either. They were a clannish lot who whispered among themselves. He suspected that they'd been planted, and they still looked just as green as they had back in August. It looked as if they weren't going to change color at all.

"Hell," the tulip leaf thought, "even the larches had the decency to do that (even if they did drop their needles the way a mangy retriever sheds fur).

You may think that all leaves fall about the same way, but this is not so. There are styles and styles, and some leaves because of their shape or size are better suited for one technique than another. Most of the birch leaves, the tulip leaf recalled, sort of sputtered to the ground, drilling holes in the air like serrated drill bits.

"It was pretty when they did it right," he had to admit, "but there wasn't much art to it."

The maples and sweet gums favored a slow spiral, a windmilling glide. With any kind of tail wind, they could really cover some ground.

"No guts, but a nice style," the leaf conceded. In fact, most of the leaves that had actually made it onto the surface of the pond were maple leaves. He'd watched the maples closely because maple and tulip leaves have a lot in common: wide bodies, sharp lobes. He had watched the maples *very* closely because if the wind was right, he thought he had a pretty good chance of reaching the pond himself. It made a good target, something to shoot for.

The oaks were an undisciplined lot, a disappointment mostly. Oh, sure, some of them made a good jump, the round-lobed kind especially. A few had introduced some nice variations, and a couple had made especially good combination dives.

But the pin oaks were something else again, something worthless. They just tumbled to the ground without dignity. Some of them just curled up and dropped like acorns. The tulip had expected more of an oak, more dignity.

There had been three frosts since the first, two of them serious. Then the rains hit, and the tulip leaves started going down. The ground directly beneath the tree was stained yellow where they had fallen.

It was the rain, of course. Wet leaves don't have a chance. They just fall without grace or dignity, drop like colored icicles. It was a hard fate, an undistinguished end, and the leaf had held on with every fiber in his petiole, waiting for the right moment.

It was hard to hold on, harder by the hour, and the tulip leaf didn't know if he could hold much longer. Several times he'd felt himself beginning to go. But each time he'd rallied and held.

"Just a little longer," he thought. "The rain's stopped and the wind should pick up as soon as the front clears. Just a little longer, now."

He tried to ease himself into a better position, but of course, he couldn't. Leaves can't move. He tried not to think of all the little things that could go wrong. The branches that might be in the way. The treacherous eddies that could start him tumbling.

He tried to clear his mind and think about nothing except the pond. And when he found he could not concentrate on the pond any longer, he thought about nothing except holding on.

"Only a little longer, now," he promised himself. "I'll drop if I have to because I'm not afraid to drop. But I want to make that pond, if I can, because it is all I can do. If I can just hold on. Hold on . . .

"Just a little longer."

But it wasn't a little longer. It was a lot longer. Past the point of stubbornness; almost past the point of pride. Finally he heard it. The sound of wind, sighing through the hemlocks across the valley. Then he felt it, almost before he was ready for it, the wind nudging him. Other leaves started down.

"I'm going to aim for that gap between those two limbs," he thought after the gust had passed. "If I make it, I've got a good shot at the pond."

He heard the wind again and started to count. One butternut . . . two butternuts . . . three butternuts . . . four . . . The wind caught him broadside, loosening his grip, almost pulling him free. Leaves filled the air.

"The next one will do it," he said aloud but to himself. "And I'm glad that I was able to hold on." He said this aloud, too. Then he gave himself to what was coming and to what he had to do. He gave himself completely.

From across the valley, the hemlocks whispered among themselves. The leaf began to count.

The bass was sluggish, lazy with the winter that was already in the water. It would be moving into deeper water soon, would have moved before this, but the rain had made the surface warm. That was why it had delayed.

A shadow passed across the fish's eyes, and something hit the surface of the pond just ahead of its snout. Despite the sluggishness, despite the fact that leaves had been hitting the pond for weeks, the bass went for it.

Bass are stupid fish.

Spent Shot Shell

IT WAS THE PUP who actually found it. He'd just discovered digging, and in the process, in the matted leaves beside the ridgetop road, he uncovered the old shotgun shell.

I traded him a stick for it. Both of us figured we'd gotten
the best of the deal.

I studied the artifact—casually at first, growing more interested by degrees. With an ungloved hand, I removed the
accumulation of many autumns, trying to be gentle, trying
not to add to the damage inflicted by time.

It was spent, of course, an empty shell. A loaded shotgun shell feels solid, heavy in your hand. It makes you want
to close your fist around it, savoring its potency. But this shell
inspired nothing but curiosity.

The weight said impotence. The weight said, there was
a time, long ago. But you missed it. I lifted the shell to my
nose anyway, in defiance of reason and time, but none of the
sweet and sour smell of burnt powder remained to reward
my nose or tickle my fancy.

It's funny how you do that—lift a shell to your nose,
sniff. It's funny how the incense of burnt power ignites
memories and feelings that go deeper than memory. It's the
kind of smell that goes well with autumn—with boots that
know where to bend, setters that know how close to work,
and a gunstock that understands precisely where to fall on a
shoulder. It's a good smell, but maybe you have to like it.

The shell resting in my palm smelled only of earth, the

only evidence to an event that had occurred here a long time ago—beyond the reach of memory, perhaps beyond the reach of my years. But maybe, just *maybe* it was not beyond recall. Could the elements of the drama that had unfolded here an age ago be pieced together? Was there enough evidence at hand to disclose the story of what happened; and if there wasn't, could I muster enough imagination to fill the gaps?

I studied the shell with heightened interest, searching for facts to anchor the foundation of a story.

It was a paper shell, a clear token of age. Plastic shells commanded the market by the time John Kennedy took the oath of office. The top had been violated by some rodent's teeth, but what remained showed clearly the folded pleats of a "star crimp"—not the narrow lip of the older roll crimp.

"All right, let's be conservative," I thought. "Let's say late fifties or early sixties. The shell might have lasted in somebody's drawer until much later, but let's say 1960. That would make it at least thirty years old."

The color was indeterminable, all printed legends and dye leached free by the oak leaves that had entombed it. No help there. I turned the shell on end, rubbed the base clean of dirt and corrosion and strained to decipher the information etched in brass.

"Peters" was clearly stamped across the top. "Victor," across the bottom. The number on the right side read "16." The legend inscribed to the right of the dented primer was illegible. But I could recall it from memory—from a host of forbidden forays to an uncle's workbench where the instruments of autumn were stored. The legend was: "Made in the U.S.A."

An appreciative whistle passed my lips. The pup raised his head, regarding me curiously, but returned to the stick.

"A Peters. Well, what do you know," I mused. The Peters ammunition company was a venerable name among sportsmen, spoken with as much reverence as Winchester or Colt. It was a name many know now only from old calendars and from wooden packing crates that decorate gunrooms and fetch ridiculous prices at auction.

"So this man shot Peters." That would make him older

than younger, I'd guess. A person who'd reached the age
when a shot that is fired is done so with deliberateness and
care; when a man may take a season and more to use a single
box of shells.

"And a sixteen-gauge shell. That's interesting. That's very
interesting."

Sixteens were never popular locally. Farmers who often
found reason to vent their anger on varmints wanted a shotgun chambered to keep pace with their wrath. Their choice
was the larger twelve or even ten gauge. Waterfowlers and
deer hunters, too, favored these bore sizes for their greater
load capacity. The ten and the twelve were meat-and-potatoes
guns; guns for a man who puts objective in the forefront of
his thinking.

On the other side of sixteen, there was the twenty
gauge—an upland gun, a gentleman's gun. Twenties were
light and quick. Easy to carry, easy to shoot, and if they didn't
throw a very big pattern of shot, well, that just made it all the
more sporting, didn't it? The twenty was a sportsman's gun.

But the sixteen was a serious gun, a hunter's gun. It was
the kind of gun used by a man who took hunting seriously
enough to see it through. A person who knew that there is
only one way to hunt, and that is to hunt well. Anything less
is frivolous; anything more is artless.

A sixteen is a hunter's gun, and a hunter is someone
who understands that means and end are inseparable,
are one.

The shell did not disclose what kind of shot it had
housed—but it hinted. It was a low brass shell, light on shot,
light on powder—the kind of shell used for upland
game—rabbits, squirrels, quail, grouse, woodcock . . . maybe
pheasant. It could have housed anything from the size of the
large, no-nonsense number 4 and 5 shot, to 6, 7, 8, all the
way down to number 9—the woodcock hunter's special.
Those were the options. Some were easily eliminated.

It was unlikely that the man was shooting 4s or 5s.
These were heavy loads, knockdown loads used when dis-
tances were long—and they were most often housed in a
high brass shell.

Number 6 shot was certainly a possibility. Six was popular, versatile, and a particularly good load for rabbit or pheasant. Eights were popular in the quail-rich South but unpopular locally. Nines? Yes, nine shot could not be discounted—if the person was hunting woodcock.

But would someone who shot a sixteen shoot nines? No . . . I don't think so. A sporting man, someone who specialized in hunting woodcock might fire nothing else. Woodcock are honest birds. If you tag them, they go down. But number nine shot isn't versatile. It doesn't offer any range, and if it is your sad fortune to hit a rabbit well at close range with a load of nines, dinner will be a tedious affair. A hunter, I guessed, wouldn't use a load that wasn't versatile or a load that compromised his reach or his dinner.

That left seven and a half, the classic grouse load. Could the man have been hunting grouse? I studied the habitat, trying to see it as it was a quarter of a century ago.

The woods would have been younger, thicker; the grape tangles crowning the canopy, lower. The overgrown orchard on the south side of the road would have been a field then, a place to find rose hips, a place to dust and absorb the stingy warmth of a winter sun. Yes, grouse were a definite possibility. But so were rabbits!

Heads or tails; call it in the air. I decided to deal with the game problem later, but a decision still had to be made concerning shot size.

I looked down at the shell, seeking guidance, but there was none. I'd have to rely on intuition. I'd have to make my best judgment.

"The man would have shot sixes," I concluded. "Because the man was a hunter, and a hunter must be versatile, and six is good for grouse and rabbit. If he had a twelve gauge, I don't know which way I'd decide—but because he shot over a sixteen, I must believe that the man used sixes."

There were still two questions left unresolved. What did he shoot at and what sort of gun did he carry? But before moving farther onto the metaphysical bridge I was building between an event and its evidence, I reviewed what I knew or suspected.

A hunter had shot at something, here, about thirty years ago. He hunted upland game. He carried a versatile but un-popular-sized shotgun. He fired ammunition that branded him an older man.

I looked to the spot where the dog had found the shell, one shell. It had lain in the middle of the road—a narrow island flanked by deep ruts. I walked over to the spot, where another man had stood, and tried to work things through. I decided to tackle the gun problem first.

"O.K.," I decided, "let's start with the obvious and try to find fault with it."

The gun was probably a double; a side-side double. When you say sixteen gauge, you say double in the same breath. The evidence said the same thing.

Chances are, the man fired at something from the road. If he had been shooting an autoloader or a pump, the spent cartridge would have been thrown by the mechanism. It *might* have landed right in the center of the road (if the fellow was standing at a right angle to the road—firing at something to the left or right), but chances are better that an autoload or pump would have thrown the shell wide, into the flanking growth.

If the man had been shooting a double, he would have broken the gun, removed the spent shell by hand, and let it fall where he stood. He would have done this if his aim had been true. He would have done this if his aim had failed— marked the spot where the test of his skills had occurred.

A sportsman who had missed might have thrown the shell in pique or disgust. But this man was a hunter. He would have respected the skills of his quarry and acknowl-edged his own limits. He would not have surrendered to his-trionics in the aftermath of so serious a drama.

It's possible that the man had not fired from the road, that he'd spotted something, walked to flush, and fired. But if that was so, he still returned to the road, and he still carried a double. And very deliberately, he had replaced a spent shell with a live one. The man hunted from the road. Why?

The wind blew chill. It picked up some leaves, and the pup chased them. The pup had energy to burn.

"He was an old man," I recalled, understanding. "He hunted from the road."

The pup was getting bored now. The shell had been forgotten; the stick was a pile of splinters. She trotted into the second growth, searching for mischief and wonders.

"He had a dog!" I realized suddenly. "He had a dog, and the dog worked the cover for him. Of course!"

Now the hard question. What was it that he had hunted here? I studied the habitat, using my mind to peel away the years. Take away the hickory and maples. There would have been overgrown fields; panic grass and blackberry tangles to the south of the road; woodland on the right—not much different than it appears now except, perhaps, for a little more understory.

The front-runners were rabbit, grouse, woodcock. Pheasant are not common in the hills of the Jersey Highlands, and bobwhite quail are absent. I dismissed the notion of a squirrel out of its habitat.

Woodcock was the least likely of the possibilities. The road was on top of the ridge. Woodcocks prefer the lower, wetter areas. Grouse? Yes, grouse was still a possibility. They were and are pretty common most years. And a double sixteen is an exceptional grouse gun, light, fast—a gun directed instead of aimed, which is perfect because a grouse doesn't give you time to aim. A man who knew how to use one could get off two shots as fast as most people get off one—and a man who knew grouse would know the need to get off a second shot even before the first had failed.

I think I wanted it to be a grouse, so I let it be one for a time, . . . but I knew in my head, if not my heart, that the truth led elsewhere.

A hunter who carried the weight of many seasons with him, who hunted from the road, and who carried number six shot in his chamber. "No, it probably wasn't a grouse." A grouse is a younger man's bird, a bird for legs that never tire and reflexes that are unsheathed by time.

I looked toward the field. "A rabbit, then. His dog was running a rabbit—a rabbit he'd found in the field." The hunter had positioned himself on the road where he thought the rabbit would cross—a place that offered a clear shot.

With the great patience of a master hunter, he had waited. With all the skills that he had gained and polished he had followed the chase. In a moment frozen in time, the gun of a hunter brought the man to bear. He fired one shot. He lifted the empty shell that was still warm and let it fall to mark the spot where this thing had happened. It happened here just as I have told it.

But did he get the rabbit?

Why, I don't know. How could I possibly know?

This Thing of Mine and Yours

HE WAS STANDING in the doorway, a brown-eyed man with an earnest way of looking at you. He was dressed like a hunter.

"Hello, Mr. Dunne," he said, extending his hand, giving me his name. The name didn't take, but the hand received mine. It was a good handshake. It said what the eyes said.

"You might remember me . . . ," he began, and I did remember him, now that he mentioned it. When I had first come to the farm, he had introduced himself, explained that he hunted an adjacent property, and asked whether he could have permission to hunt ours too. The answer was no.

"I noticed you've posted the property," he continued, "and a few of your signs are out of place."

The news didn't surprise me. That particular property line hadn't been posted in five years. The old signs were long gone; the boundary had more twists and turns than a soap opera story line. Projecting the boundary was a matter of locating trees bearing old nail wounds and seeking out the buried remains of old stone walls. At times, it was a matter of conjecture.

"There's only one or two that are misplaced," he explained, and "I'm not asking you to take them down. But if you'd like, I'll walk the line with you so that we both have our bearing straight."

It was a generous offer and generously put.

"Let me find my boots," I said.

The day was warm, as warm as the day I had posted—taken a staple gun, a wad of fluorescent orange signs, and a marking pencil and stalked down to the border. I found the corner easily enough. There was an old rock wall. There was fresh surveyor tape. I confronted an old white oak studded with nails, covered them with a sign, and placed the gun on its face, firing four times.

Spink, the device said. *Spink, Spink, Spink.* It sounded good in the still, woodland air: definitive, no nonsense—the first point of a line to be drawn in the trees. I fired two more rounds, dead center, to finish it off.

Spink, Spink.

"Take that, you would-be trespassers, you heinous, un-law-abiding transgressors of other people's property," I felt more than thought. I stepped back to admire my handiwork, feet spaced wide, hands on hips. The staple gun heavy and cold in my grip.

It's a funny thing, the posting ritual. "It's a 'male thing,'" Linda said, shaking her head, giving her attention back to her garden, and maybe she is right. It is also an ancient thing, this separation of "mine" from "yours," and creatures have been doing it ever since the concept of "self."

Some creatures, like birds, get their territorial point across through song. The mockingbird sitting on our chimney sings a ring around its personal space, saying in many different bird languages, "This is mine, and yours is somewhere else."

Coyotes draw a bead down a raised hind leg and fire a burst of urine at a strategic bush. Dogs do the same thing. Bears etch their brand on trees, reaching up to rake the bark, leaving a message that reads: "If you can't reach this high, you are standing in the wrong place, Bub."

Humans draw up contracts; file deeds, copyrights, patents; plant flags; erect fences and walls; make reservations for dinner, the racketball court, a seat on a flight to Chicago. And they raise a staple gun and leave their fluorescent brands on trees.

It *sometimes* happens that what is "mine" overlaps or conflicts with what is "yours." When this happens, many things are possible. One of them is peaceful resolution.

We fought our way through the greenbrier and the brush that gains a foothold on fallow land. Brush is the shock troop of forest. As we walked, I learned a little more about the man whose territory bordered mine. He was a chemist. He and his son-in-law had hunted this land for many years. It was the only place in New Jersey he hunted. His manner and his talk convinced me that he took it seriously.

Others, unfortunately, do not. The opening day of deer season finds every bozo with a shotgun stalking the landscape, drawing the angst of landowners and serious hunters alike.

I recall the two guys who plainly shot a doe from the road in front of our house two years ago. This itself is illegal, of course. So is shooting a deer on somebody else's property without permission.

I recall the guy who showed up one day with a great big smile and told me what a great big favor he and his friends were going to do for me by hunting my property. I didn't care for him or his approach. I liked him even less the next year when he came back and pointed out that it was my obligation to let him "cull the herd" for the "health and well-being of deer populations," or some stupid euphemism like that. Fact is, I knew as much about deer management as he did, and I also knew something he had apparently overlooked. I'm not stupid. I knew precisely why he and his "friends" wanted to hunt the property, and it had nothing to do with game management. I give points for honesty.

"This sign," the brown-eyed hunter said, "cuts the corner a little. I figured you put it here just for emphasis because you have signs beyond. It's O.K. to leave it."

Actually, what had happened was that I had found old nails in that tree and slapped a sign on it. Later, I discovered what appeared to be a survey cut and tore down the signs I had just put up. This one had been overlooked.

He showed me where his son-in-law would be on opening day, a tree stand just above the old rock wall. "We don't shoot into your property," he assured, and his expression said this was so. The fact is, both his son-in-law's stand and his own were placed on major deer trails that stitched the property line. Our side was thick and brushy; their side was

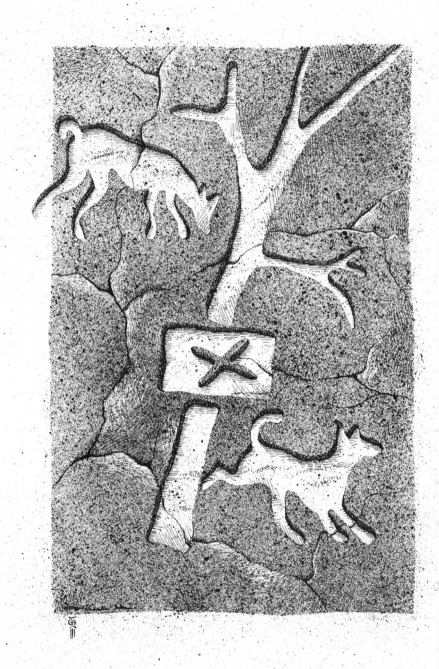

open, would offer a better, more confident shot. His promise and his expression were backed by pragmatism.

He showed me where a buck had been marking its territory. There was a "rub" where the animal had used its antlers to polish a young maple down to sapwood. There was a bare scrape where the animal had left its mark.

In turn, I showed him a sapsucker working the trunk of a wild cherry. It was late in the season for "saps." He donned my binoculars and trained them on the bird.

There was one other sign out of place, another I had meant to take down but forgotten. It was placed on the tree where his deer stand was positioned. The stand mantled the rock wall, but the wall itself was set back from the survey cut. He was in bounds; my sign was not.

"You can leave it up," he assured. "Just as long as we're both comfortable with the boundary."

"No," I said, reaching for the sign, tearing it off, bending it into quarters. "It's a mistake, and it might just confuse somebody later."

It was getting late. The woods had taken on that smoky cast that winter woodlands do when the sun draws down. We had walked our mutual boundary. Each of us knew where the other stood, and we were content.

"If I see someone trespassing on your property," he said, "would you like me to tell them to leave."

"Yes," I said, "I'd appreciate that." It wasn't something he had to do, and it actually worked against him. Somebody walking the property stood a good chance of sending a deer his way.

Boundaries are ancient things. Maybe reciprocity is, too. "If you hit a deer," I said, "and it runs onto our side, you can go get it without having to get my permission." There was no guarantee that I'd be home, and somehow I knew he wouldn't abuse the privilege.

"Thanks," he said, extending his hand once more—an ancient gesture. "See," it says, "I hold no weapon."

"You're welcome," I said, taking it.

Epistle to Be Left in the Leaves

(With Apologies to Archibald MacLeish)

A SCORE OF YEARS have passed since the laws were changed in the town where I grew up, putting an end to that most hallowed of autumn rituals—burning leaves. The passing was greeted with enthusiasm by lobbying asthmatics, hardly noticed by others. Now, a generation has grown up, and nary a nostril has flared to the tang of smoldering leaves, the burned essence of autumn. This is a tragedy.

The lore of leaf burning is precious. Unless recorded, it will soon be forgotten—a lost art like milking the cow, tamping the charge, or changing a typewriter ribbon. This then is an epistle to be left in the leaves. For any who might find it; for future generations so that you, who open this writing, may know that we of this age knew craft.

Think back you homeowners, you high-rise and condo-dwellers with suburban roots, think back. Recall how it was. You woke early on that blessed Saturday morning, and the smell of bacon filled the air. There was quickness in your movements, eagerness in your step. Through the chink in the bathroom window's caulking, you felt the chill in the air, and beyond the frost-etched glass, naked branches of trees stood unmoving against the sky. Conditions were perfect!

Under the shower, your muscles flexed with anticipation of pleasant labor. There was always enough hot water on this day no matter how many kids had gone off to Pop Warner football games or the Frosh car wash. Chins never got nicked on this morning. Shoelaces never broke. Car keys were never lost. And coffee was always just right.

The kids would call to ask permission to spend the night with friends. Long-standing dinner plans with some boring couple across town would fall through. And you and your spouse would be left to contemplate a long evening together free of commitments. Such was the magic of this day.

Soon, you stood at the edge of your property sizing up the yard. It was nothing at all like the dreary contemplation of cutting the lawn. Hell, any joy to be found in that mindless chore had the brains beaten out of it before the daffodils wilted. No, this was different. Very different.

Each year, the debate seemed fresh in your mind. "Should I rake it all at once, row by row, or divide the lawn into sections and tackle them one at a time? And every year you made the right choice.

Do you remember how the rake felt in your hands? How the handle was shiny with use, stained dark in two places where your hands (and only your hands) fell. You could have used work gloves, of course, but you did not.

"Only a barbarian would use gloves on **this** rake."

Do you remember that first sweep, how the metal tines vibrated in pitch, how the leaves fled before you? The old rhythm just came of itself, unbidden, and the rustle of your labors filled the air. With a sideways glance (and just pride), you noted how you still set the best pace in the neighborhood. By lunch, the job was done—the lawn unveiled; the leaves piled deep at the curb. And I ask you, when did tomato sandwiches ever taste so good? After lunch, there was time to pay some bills, read the cover story in *Time* magazine, and maybe catch a little bit of college football on the tube. And then, through some great instinct, you knew that the moment had arrived. It was time to start the burning.

You walked toward the curb with the eyes of the neighborhood upon you, testing the wind with your cheek, tacking to arrive on the windward side of the pile. The match would snap and flair. Even gopher matches (You know: the pocket matchbook kind? Light one, *go fer* another) would strike first time, every time.

The leaves would smoke, a silky blue plume chased by a yellow flame. And the neighborhood kids would gather to witness as the smoke curled skyward filling the air with the tang of burning leaves, the true smell of autumn.

At this magic moment, the humblest suburban dweller is transformed. For this one Saturday out of the year, every homeowner becomes Druid for a Day, and the flames that crackle at the curb glow with the fervor of the finest pyre kindled on the most hallowed Celtic hilltop.

I remember how proud I was to witness the burning: proud that I was old enough and my brothers weren't, proud that my father was an initiate to such an important ritual. I remember how skillfully he probed with his rake where the flames had passed, exposing leaves hidden beneath the ash, putting them to righteous fire. I recall his trick of gathering burning leaves in his rake and moving them down the pile. Every place he touched burst into fresh flames.

He always knew precisely where to place the burning rake, my father. And he never needed more than one match to burn the whole lot (even when there were separate piles). Such was my father's skill, the best leaf burner in the neighborhood.

When I was older, when I had learned "responsibility," they let me burn the leaves. Of course, I had to rake them, too, but I had to do that even before I learned responsibility. Being allowed to burn the leaves is a suburban right of passage. Right up there with being allowed to stay out after dark; equal in weight to being allowed to borrow the family car.

For the very first time in your life, you were permitted to carry matches. That's a grown-up thing to do. For the first time in your life, you had to resist the temptation to run through the smoke. That's a little kid thing to do.

This was *your* fire, the first blaze of a newly ordained suburban Druid priest. If just one little thing went wrong! If just one stupid little kid ran through the leaves or threw paper on the fire, it would be a whole year before you got the chance to carry matches again. That was for sure.

The fires are gone now, excised by ordinance. Burning leaves were an affront to civilization, an irritant and a hazard to sensitive lungs. Now, autumn's annual tribute is mulched and taken by the wind or stuffed into collection bags like common trash. In some communities, the piles lie long in the gutter waiting for the municipal truck to arrive. Hoses suck them up like so much dirt off the carpet.

And raking leaves isn't what it used to be now that they've taken the fire out of it. The task has become a chore, a bother like putting up the storm windows and cleaning the gutters.

My coffee was weak this morning, and the frost got the last tomatoes. In half an hour, I have to shower and dress for some stupid party that's an hour's drive, and I can't find the car keys.

The lore of leaf burning is no longer of this age. But I have written it down as I remember it. So that the wisdom may be preserved. So that you who might find it will know and understand.

I will place this writing in one of the bags I leave on the curb, where, no doubt, it will lie, wrapped in impregnable plastic for a thousand years waiting for a hand to find it— some kindly publisher perhaps, who, pressed for another essay to fill up an assembled collection, may print it.

Mus Ado about Something

AT FIRST, there was just the barest hint of a sound, the sort of noise that exerts enough leverage to brings heads up and leave them hanging. "Must be the wind," I hypothesized, surrendering to the lure of that timeless red herring.

"Windy," I said to the eyes peering at me over the top of some mystery writer's literary probe. The wifely eyes crinkled skeptically but fell back onto the text.

"I hope the 'wind' has enough sense to take a powder, or it's a pogrom for sure," I mused. But "the wind" had other ideas.

From the depths of the shadows that live in basements came the unmistakable scamper of rodent feet followed by the sound that very sharp incisors make when a sunflower seed is being husked. The dog raised his ears, then his head.

Scampers became scuttles became rustles became a scuffle! A sharp "squeak" was punctuated by the equally unmistakable "plop" of some dislodged creature hitting the landing. The dog "whoofed" a challenge and raced to do his doggy duty. Reluctantly, I glanced over toward the reading chair to meet the eyes I knew would be waiting for mine to arrive. The message they flashed was easy to read.

"We, meaning 'you' (meaning 'me') have to do something about that, meaning 'them' (meaning 'the mice')."

I nodded. The eyes had it. In the divvying up of household tasks, rodent control had fallen within my fief.

"I'll set some traps," I said.

I'm a peaceful man, a patient man. Live and let live, that's me. Our household is uncommonly tolerant of live-in critters—which is good for our sake (and theirs). We reside in an indefensible old farmhouse. Critters come with the turf.

The foundation of Linda's and my tolerance antedates our residence and partnership. Mine came of age in Cape May, New Jersey, where I lived with flying squirrels in my closet.

Let me clarify that. *I* lived in a *room*; the squirrels occupied the closet (and the walls, and attic, and assorted nooks and crannies). But in eleven years of cohabitation, I never once evoked the eviction rights accorded by nature to larger, more powerful creatures.

"Heck," I reasoned, "better squirrels than wolverines."

I even maintained this philosophical equanimity after the furry little nihilists chewed the bejeebers out of a dozen wool sweaters and trashed my only sports jacket.

"How often does a naturalist really need a jacket?" I decided.

My wife is equally nonplussed in the face of mammalian invaders—my wife who once dragged a snarling coyote pup into her mom's kitchen by the scruff of the neck and asked whether she could keep it. Twenty years' residency in places like Alaska, Alberta, and Wyoming instill lots of critter savvy in a person. After being treed by bears and cornered in a cloth-top jeep by a bruised and unamused moose, my wife could probably teach a Ghandi a thing or two about passive resistance.

One summer morning, after finishing a pile of left-overnight dishes, Linda discovered a very wet and very annoyed red bat at the bottom of the rinse sink. Bats must drop from a perch in order to get airborne. Once grounded, they're stuck. While this explains *why* a bat was lying in the sink, how it came to be there was and remains a mystery. What did Linda do? Picked the critter up in a towel and hung it out to dry.

What else do you do with a wet bat?

Our recent fuss with the *Mus* had been brewing since late November. Linda and I returned from a month's absence to a house that smelled like a hamster cage and was carpeted in things that looked like caraway seeds (but weren't). The onset of cold weather had very clearly sent a host of small rodents in search of winter quarters, and the old farmhouse, in our absence, had won unprecedented favor.

By and large, mice are congenial, unobtrusive creatures. They like attics, baseboard heaters, and walls—all of which are places Linda and I rarely frequent. Since we were plainly set on monopolizing the daylight hours, the mice cheerfully elected to take the night shift. Some might think that this arrangement would have tempted our furry minions to ride roughshod in the kitchen. But in the spirit of conciliation, they discreetly avoided the place, directing their culinary favor, instead, upon the dog's food bowl—all in all not a bad arrangement. The dog was a bit put out, but he's smart enough to know who it is that puts the food in that bowl. In the end, he sided with us.

So we and the mice came to terms. We accepted a nominal amount of traffic in the walls, and they could pretty much count on our benign indifference. This harmony might have continued indefinitely except the mice discovered our stock of wild birdseed. Overnight, it seemed, the entire populace fell victim to "the devil seed," and the fabric of our peaceful society was shattered.

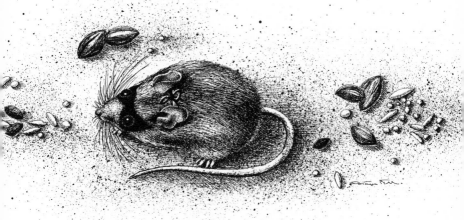

Soon, seed-crazed mice could be seen at almost any hour racing from room to room, cheek pouches bursting with pilfered Special Mix. Little caches of thistle seed began turning up inside shoes, coat pockets, drawers . . . even between the bed sheets. On one momentous evening, a seed cache hidden under the right front burner went up like an ammo dump.

The skittering in the walls at night increased to freeway proportions. Squabbles over seed rights and baseboard rights-of-way became commonplace. Domestic violence was clearly on the rise. Then, on a cold night just before Christmas, we heard the sound we dreaded. Instead of a mousy skitter in the attic, there was a scuttle, a heavy-footed scuttle—Thumper in rat's clothing.

"Uh, oh," the eyes that I could not see in the dark room, said loud and clear. "Uh, oh."

We waited until after the holidays (a humanitarian gesture) before engaging in hostilities. Our defensive arsenal consisted of eight new McGill Never-miss mouse traps (products of a recent arms buildup) and a pair of trusty old Victors—sole representatives of our peacetime trap fleet. But intelligence estimates suggested that even this beefed-up fleet was low on firepower. Accordingly, I went out to the barn, reached into a corner of discarded bric-a-brac, and pulled a rusty old battlewagon from the heap—a real knuckle-cracker of a rat trap.

Properly peanut-buttered, our little battle group was deployed in a preestablished defense perimeter. Two elements in the snap-trap class went into the kitchen; two more guarded our flank down in the basement. The main battle group, two Never-misses and the veteran Victors, went right in harm's way—right around the birdseed canister.

Holding the high ground in the attic was ol' knuckle-cracker with two snap-traps serving escort duty. Frankly, I didn't know what they might face up there. But if Thumper came out of hiding and it came down to a firefight, they'd be on their own.

The night was windy, mercifully muffling the sound of skitters, scuffles, or things that go snap in the night. Before dawn, before coffee, I went down to learn the sad tidings.

As expected, the kitchen traps were untouched; likewise the pair in the basement. But around the seed, it was carnage and mayhem. Four traps; four mice. Two were *Mus*, and two were white-foots, *Paramiscus leucopus*—clear evidence that our internal insurrection had been orchestrated from outside. In the attic, one trap held another white-footed, a real buster, too.

A great victory? Only in part. Ol' knuckle-cracker had tangled with something in the attic that had taken the bait, a full broadside, and then taken its leave. Whatever else the attic thumper might be, it was a wiser creature now. We may have won a battle. But by the signs, it seemed all but certain that we were embroiled in a long, long campaign.

Season's First Snow

IT WAS RALPH BROKAW, a toll taker on duty at the Delaware Water Gap, who is credited with having seen the first flakes touch down in New Jersey. Though stationed on the Pennsylvania side (technically out of bounds), Ralph felt winter touch the back of his hand as he handed four dollars change to Lisa Stevenson of Dearborn, Michigan, who was en route to a job interview in Teaneck.

By the time he'd broken Bruce Zatkow's twenty, peeled the double-faced tape from the back of the Susan B. Anthony that had, until recently, been mounted on the dashboard of Irene Musica's vintage Capri, and handed Joe Olshefski his receipt, the swirling cloud of flakes had jumped the river. He looked at his watch, noting that he still had over two hours till the shift change at three.

In the amount of time that it took to tell Tim Yamashita how to get to the Lincoln Tunnel, Mount Tammany was little more than a smoky shadow behind a curtain of snow.

Just down the road, at the Water Gap Visitor Center, National Park Service Interpretive Naturalist Roxanne Kaiser heard the tire noise of the eighteen-wheelers go from whine to a whisper. She crossed to a window overlooking the river; her thoughts were on the skis waxed and waiting on the porch.

At Belvidere Elementary School, Miss Anne Baxter, art teacher, was powerless to stop the stampede to the windows in response to Archie Bianco's catalytic shout of "Hey, look it's snowin'!" In something under fifteen seconds, the plate glass medium was a mosaic of hand prints, nose prints, and vapor clouds. It hadn't occurred to anybody (yet) that tomorrow was Saturday. What a waste of a snowfall.

Downstairs, behind the door marked "Principal," Joe Rowley sat trying to decide whether to call for early dismissal or gamble on a dusting. In the time it took to reach a decision, from 1:09 to 1:14, the parking lot went from black to white—clear evidence that early dismissal was a defensible option. At 1:15 he picked up the phone . . .

In Newton, four-year veteran of the force Tony Artiglaire was listening to Sylvia Snyder explain (again) how she "was just approaching the intersection, traveling at a very safe speed, when the light suddenly changed, but" (although she applied the brakes in plenty of time) "the car just kept going forward." It might have interested them to know that exchanges very similar to this one were also going on at intersections in Branchville, Succasunna, Milton, Hamburg, Oldwick, Stanhope, Hackettstown, Washington, Frenchtown, Hopatcong, and a place known locally as Ross's Corner. Given the nature of cause and effect, some fundamental principles governing things like bodies in motion, space and matter, and the bonding properties of rubber and ice, this was all very understandable.

These same principles were key causal agents in the friendship that developed between Rebecca Spielman and Susan Brown in the Bridgwater Common's parking lot. In the forty minutes that it took to unhook bumpers, they discovered a whole host of shared interests and acquaintances (a list that merely began with Ray Sayre, agent, State Farm Insurance).

Around the corner, at the Automotive Center, Joe Leo pulled the left rear wheel from the sixth car he'd fitted for snow tires since noon and wondered, again, why it is that people always wait till the last minute. His boss, with a fistful of orders, started to walk toward Joe's bay, and Joe knew, just knew, that he was going to be asked to work overtime. It's not that he couldn't use the money. It's just that it was Friday night, and he had plans . . .

So did Mike O'Mally, owner of O'Mally Oldsmobile,

and they were rapidly falling through. Sales had been terrible, *terrible*, and his dealership was on the ropes. He'd gambled heavily on pulling off a big, one-day sales blitz scheduled for Saturday. He stood watching snow drape the rows of this year's models and last year's leftovers. Ignoring the members of his sales force who were trying valiantly to appear busy behind their empty desks, Mike crossed the showroom, entered his office, and dialed the bank. One minute later, the "best damn new car salesman that ever lived" was making the most important sales pitch of his life.

Pitch was very much on the mind of Micky Mutchler, aged four, or, more appropriately, the lack of it. Front lawns in Cranbury, New Jersey, aren't known for their contours, and although a fundamental understanding of sledmanship is innate in children, that doesn't help if you "don't got no hill." Unfortunately for Micky, the lack of a hill wasn't his only or most serious problem. The shiny new sled that he'd "found" in the garage wasn't supposed to make its inaugural run until *after* it arrived, special delivery, from the North Pole. To compound Micky's misfortunes, his father was just turning into the drive. A father who had been slugging it out in snow-strangled traffic for three hours.

Snow was also on the mind of Sarah Stout, resident of the Shady Oaks Convalescent Home near Medford Lakes— but at ninety-nine, her mind perpetually wandered through a great deal of snow, through memories that drifted and blew into barriers against the outside world. But given the fact that life had been reduced to a room, a bed, meals, and a TV, the memories of a long and colorful lifetime were far more compelling than reality (such as it was). And as the snow piled up unseen against the windows of her room, great drifts of memories and feelings filled her mind, and she smiled.

Manny Hannisian, owner and proprietor of Manny's body shop was smiling too. Snow always made Manny smile. So did ice and fog. While he enjoyed the beautiful, beautiful snow and a fresh cigar, he compared the considerable merits of Cancun, Honolulu, and the Costa del Sol.

"Man, I love snow," Manny said aloud, and he meant it too.

Just south of the Island Beach exit on the Garden State

Parkway, Tim Yamashita pulled into the rest area to check his bearings. In his room in Cranbury, Micky Mutchler was trying to come to grips with what to his mind was a monstrous injustice—the price of getting caught with the smoking gun.

In her kitchen in Millville, Dorothy Slack put the last tray of pfefferneusse into the oven, wiped her hands on her apron, and moved toward the window. Carolina chickadees and tufted titmice were feeding frantically, fueling up for what promised to be a bitter night.

On the other side of town, Chris Kapsa opened the porch door for her toy poodle, Mouse. Mouse, whose distaste for the white stuff was legendary, was never known to put four paws into the stuff when she could get away with three, or three when two would do. As Chris watched in mirthful admiration, Mouse minced her way toward the target zone. Shifting her weight forward, she executed a beautiful front paw stand and at the same time drew a daring little yellow figurine in the snow.

In a small house, with windows that poured their light into a fast-darkening world, Johanna Massey polished the essay she was sending off to the *New Jersey Audubon Magazine*. She listened to the sound of wind in the ancient willow. She listened to the hiss of snow falling into the Cohansey and to the sound of the river in flood. She listened with a mother's sensitive ears for the sound of the school bus that must travel all the way from Bridgeton.

Just past midnight, when Henelopen light showed plainly across Delaware Bay, a red fox walked across the empty meadows, leaving nothing but small, round tracks in the season's first snow.

Ode to Ma'am Dog

THE DOOR OPENED, throwing light onto the lawn and igniting the eyes of deer.

"Hi, guys," our neighbor Debbie chanted, "come in; season's cheer."

"What are you drinking?" asked her husband, Tom, who without waiting for a reply, reached for the usual toxin.

On the porch, there was bedlam. Labrador leaping and lusty sniffing and enough tail wagging to suggest that dogs should be considered as candidates for an alternate energy source. Prudence, the neighbors' new Labrador puppy, and our dog, Moose (who after three years still thought of himself as a puppy), were attempting a black and yellow fur fusion, and even Cally, the five-year-old, had dropped her usual reserve and thrown her ample pelt into the ring.

We were long past the "How are you"s and well into the "So what have you been doing"s before it occurred to me that there was an element missing.

"Where's Ma'am Dog?" I asked.

The silence went a long way, all the way to the abyss and wherever that leads to. It's a silence that lasts forever, and that's about how long it felt before Debbie grabbed the social initiative, reined in eternity, and brought our conversation back within earthly bounds.

"She's up on the hillside next to Hombre," she said, and unless you knew Debbie's voice, you'd never have heard the strain in it.

"Ahhh," I think I said, or some such noise, but my mind had left the conversation. It had gone off in search of the old black Lab who had pretty nearly run things at both the Zenos' place and ours.

Ma'am was a force to be reckoned with—a stately, straight-shooting Texas lady who'd left her brand on dogs and human hearts alike. I can't tell you much about Ma'am's past and less about her lineage. Debbie and Ma'am had teamed up while she, Debbie, an engineer, had been working on a project for Texas-based Exxon. I'm guessing that Ma'am's folks were working dogs, versatile beasts that could dog-paddle the great Gulf Coast marshes in search of downed waterfowl by day and fight their way through thickets by night till whatever raccoon they were running sought the mistaken safety of a tree.

I'm also only guessing when I call her a Lab. Ma'am's legs were long, her nose fox-thin, and there was little about her that resembled the blocky English Labrador bloodline—a breed of dog built like a dumpster. Her build clearly inclined itself toward the lanky, American Lab line, and it's not certain that all of her feet were in bounds.

By the time we met, Ma'am and I, she had dropped whatever bulk she may have carried in her younger years. The dog that accompanied Debbie to meet the new neighbor was already an old dog with a frosted muzzle and eyes grown misty with years.

Cally was all puppy-lumber and wiggle when I opened the door. She had a head that demanded to be petted and eyes that said "adore me." She could wrap herself around an ankle like a cat, and no matter how much attention you directed her way, she always managed to leave you with the impression that it fell short of her standards.

Ma'am was different. Ma'am stood by Debbie's side, taking my measure with a straight tail and drooped snout. After a pensive few moments, she stalked forward, stiff legged, going straight for the trouser cuff, where all that a dog needs to know about a human is found. Two sniffs were all it took, one for an assessment and one for clarification. Then she brought her eyes up, inviting my hand, and this, for a dog like Ma'am, is the final test of a human.

Some dogs like their heads rubbed; some like a hand to reach for the good scratching place behind the ear. Somehow I knew I should go for an ear, and the dreamy look spawned behind the milky way clouds across her eyes told me I'd guessed right. Ma'am and I were friends—sealed with a scratch.

Others in Ma'am's sphere of influence have not won her countenance as quickly or as easily. When Cally first set foot in Ma'am's domain his blundering puppy nose was met with a punishing set of canines. Ma'am stapled a hole right through Cally's snout, and this one, short, decisive stroke assured her dominance in the household.

I don't know what force or methods brought this message home to our dog, Moose. I only know that when the dogs came visiting, and Ma'am stalked over to Moose's food dish, the Moose gave ground.

It took time for Prudence to be initiated into the hierarchy of the pack. Maybe it was because Ma'am was getting near the end of her days. Maybe it was because Tom and Debbie went out of their way to try to enforce the peace. For whatever reason, the new puppy rode rough-shod over poor old Ma'am for a full week before Ma'am finally had enough.

Nobody really knows the circumstances, but Debbie said it happened pretty quick—a sunrise showdown out by the Zeno horse corals while Debbie was cleaning out stalls. Suddenly there was a yelp. By the time Debbie arrived on the scene, Ma'am was standing, and pup was bleeding, the result of an enamel-jacketed canine that had passed clean through the pup's nose—Ma'am's favorite shot.

If you look now, at Cally's nose and the pup's, why, the two wounds aren't off by more than a quarter of an inch. Ol' Ma'am was one straight-shooting dog, let me tell you.

In her younger years, Debbie tells me, Ma'am used to just run down rabbits, one, two, three. But by the time Ma'am and I firmed our friendship, her rabbit-running days were behind her. For some reason, Ma'am never took out after deer, and it wasn't for lack of opportunity. Deer, on our Hunterdon County, New Jersey, farm are as common as Democrats in Texas. It wasn't for lack of interest, either. Ma'am was plainly fascinated by deer. She would stand and watch them for as long as you, or they, would let her. But chase them, she would not.

Maybe it was discipline. Maybe it was something that transcended human understanding. There was, if you looked closely, a remarkable similarity in Ma'am Dog's physique and the lithesome leggyness of white-tailed deer. Maybe Ma'am thought of deer as kin.

Most likely, it was her age, because Ma'am's ancestors must have run deer with as much enthusiasm as they ran raccoons. But by the time Ma'am was nine, arthritis had crept into her hips. Though she could be coaxed into play, even into the last year of her life, her breath was labored at twelve and raspy at thirteen.

She was, for the years that spanned our friendship, an old dog who came to be an old, old dog who came more and more to enjoy evenings by the hearth. There, warmed by the coals, the raspy breaths would ease somewhat, and her legs would twitch as she chased dream rabbits through dream fields.

But let a person stand and head for the kitchen and Ma'am was right at his or her heels. Age had taken her agility but none of her craftiness. She still managed, somehow, to get two dog biscuits for every other dog's one. In fact, the last time she spent the evening in our place, we almost ran out. I had to halve the few biscuits that remained to make them go around. Ma'am saw through this subterfuge but suffered it with dignity and forgave me out of friendship.

When our company, dog and human, left that night, cleared the door, and turned left down the walk, Ma'am missed the turn, stumbling on. She stopped and stood for a time, facing the winter-darkened world alone, then retreated, heading back through our open door, heading for the light.

"Poor old Ma'am Dog," I thought as I led her out again and guided her down to the Zenos' car. Only now does it occur to me that her apparent confusion may all have been a ruse. It would have been just like Ma'am to use the guise of dotage to shed the other dogs so she could con one last dog biscuit for the ride home. It wasn't her cleverness that failed her. It was her friend and neighbor whose uptake was just too slow on the draw.

It's almost New Year's, and dog biscuits are plentiful once again. I think come New Year's Day I might walk up to the hillside and find the soft brown spot next to where Hombre sleeps and honor the memory of her craftiness with a biscuit.

The Fox Who Ran Forever

WHEN HE was certain that the shadows were only shadows, the fox stepped away from the pines and started across the cornfield. Walking, sometimes trotting, he navigated the stubble rows, testing the world around him with eyes and ears and nose—which as any red fox will tell you are the finest in the world.

The sharp, questioning nose told him that a meadow vole lay somewhere beneath the snow. But the fox had fed earlier and well. He took no notice.

The quick, intelligent eyes surveyed the hedges and hillsides—but saw nothing to account for the restlessness that tugged at his feet.

His ears still caught and held the sound that had puzzled the fox for half the night. It was a sound like the sound the stars make on cold, still nights, but louder, much louder. If you do not know this sound, it is akin to the echo of the sea trapped within a conch, but fainter—*so faint*, that only foxes and children who listen very hard can hear it. Adults who can recall something of this sound know it only as a memory awakened by dreams; the echo of an echo of a sound heard long ago.

The source of the sound lay to the east, and it seemed to align itself along a pale swath of stars that shed their cold light upon the earth. The fox discovered that as the miles fell away, the sound grew louder—going from a hum to a hiss to a whisper, so loud that it nearly drowned out the silent footfalls of a fox in the snow.

He was a large, healthy, handsome fox. His coat was a deep, rich red, white fringed and full. The tail was magnificent. His face had the chiseled sharpness that wild creatures have (and domestic creatures envy), and his eyes were button black.

When he was a much younger fox, he had been reckless and daring. Fixed in his mind were the memories of vixens chased by moonlight, rivals fought and vanquished, hounds that were outwitted, and times of famine he had survived because he had been clever (and young). Now, he was old and wise, endowed with the deep, deep wisdom that only years of adventure can engender. He was also very lucky, but this goes without saying. After all, he was alive! And this takes a measure of luck even if you are not a fox.

Years ago, he had settled in the rolling farmland that falls gradually into the Delaware River. He had remained there for no other reason except that it suited him, and until this night, he had never left it. But until this night, the stars had left the earth in peace, and now his favorite haunts lay far behind. Only the stars were familiar.

He trotted more than walked now, moving as silently as shadows cross the snow. There was a hard crust beneath the dusting of powder, and on a surface like this, a fox could run clear on till morning. A fox could run forever.

Overhead, the stars grew brighter, and the whisper grew steadily in his ears. His course carried him through pale woodlands creased by shadows, fields that lay naked to the universe, across frozen streams and frozen highways that looked like streams. He trotted easily across pastures and parking lots, across corporate lawns and backyards that slept beneath their blanket of snow.

Now and again, he would see other creatures—or they him. Many times he caught the alluring smell of rabbit or the intoxicating scent of pheasant. Several times he felt the eyes of owls upon him, and twice he encountered other foxes.

The first was another male, younger and smaller than

himself. The animal was plainly puzzled to find another fox within its territory, but more puzzled still, it seemed, by the shivering whisper that plagued its ears. The errant fox and the puzzled fox passed, but no words passed between them.

The other fox was a female, almost as old as himself. She too heard the ringing sound emanating from the heavens, but whether because she commanded some higher wisdom or because she put greater stock in more practical adventures, she ignored it. With a flash of a tail every bit as impressive as his own, the vixen trotted off, barely slowing her pace as she rounded a corner.

After a hesitation so slight that it barely deserves to be called indecision, the fox moved on—the whispered chorus growing louder in his ears, the stars still mapping a course for his eyes to follow.

"Must be getting old," he thought.

He ran more than trotted now, and he discovered as he ran that it was no longer necessary to gaze skyward to follow the path of stars. They had grown so bright that their light burned in the snow, and the course was laid before him like a highway set in silver.

He took his bearings along the tail of the Great Bear, running now, as only a fox can run, following the line that pointed straight to the single bright star just cresting the horizon. With this star in his eyes, with this star to guide him, he lengthened his stride and put the world behind.

The silver chiming grew louder, and louder, so loud, in fact, that it ceased to have a source. More and more it seemed to come from all around, seemed even to come from within.

He was close enough now to tell that the sound was made by innumerable bells dancing in the eternal wind, and he wondered how he knew this (since foxes know nothing about bells or eternity). He guessed it was because he was so close.

But there was no time even to think because he was running, now, running as only a fox can run. Faster than thought or reflex. Faster than he or any living fox has ever run before.

Faster than anything!

He was running so fast that his shadow lagged, and his

footprints fell far behind. He was running so fast that the lesser stars ran together in a blur, and their light was so bright that it flooded the eastern sky, igniting the snow in all directions.

Only the Great Star was visible now, and this was the star he steered by. This was the star he sought. Straight as a line drawn between two stars, he raced, faster than the light that reached out to claim it.

But the star held true, and he held true to his star. Over fences and fields, through villages and towns and half a million dreams he ran. Straight on till morning.

There were crows in the sky when he slowed to walk, and he stopped, finally, next to a snow-covered sand box. He sat for several moments, panting, studying the split-level ranch with the redwood deck situated on a one-acre lot. Calmly but cautiously (because he was a wild creature), he made his way up to the sliding glass doors that opened onto the den.

Across the room was a tree that blazed with many lights and from whose limbs a host of silver bells dangled. Atop the tree was a star. At the base of the tree was a pile overflowing with presents. And a large black dog. And a human boy of two or three. Clenched very tightly in the boy's arms, half hidden beneath the tree, was another red fox with black button eyes.

The dog and the boy were asleep, but the fox who was held seemed very much awake and very much alive, and the two foxes stared silently at each other for a long time, sharing thoughts that only two foxes might understand.

Chickadees, weak from cold, swept down upon the nearby feeder, scolding the fox loudly. The dog opened his eyes, saw the fox, and growled. But the fox ignored him. There was so little time, you see, and so much that had to be passed on. The fox that was held would have years to communicate this wisdom to the boy, but the fox who was not held, and who had never been held, had only the time that was left. That time is never enough.

Later, but not much later, when the doors were drawn

back and a near apoplectic dog was finally let out to attend to business, he didn't make his usual beeline to the corner of the yard. Instead, he ran circles around the patio, sniffing lustily, obliterating, in his haste, the telltale depression next to the door. The single set of tracks, running one before the other, straight as a line drawn between stars that led right to the doorway, was noticed by no one.